When processing grief, some men can [hide?] their emotions, and instead seek to bury them. [That doesn't?] hold up for long when one is experiencing an excruciating internal [pain. A?] roadmap is required, showing them how they might live again.

The brave fathers who authored this anthology have paved a healing path for others who've suffered the wrenching pain of a child's passing. They've been through it and survived—some are even thriving.

- Mark Ireland, author of *Soul Shift*, *The Persistence of the Soul*, and co-founder of Helping Parents Heal

§

In my work with Helping Parents Heal and through my personal engagements with my clients, I have noticed a troubling trend: the narrative of grief is predominantly voiced by women.

Helping Fathers Heal is a beacon of hope in this landscape. This book is not just a guide; it's a permission slip for fathers to embrace their grief fully and authentically. It understands that men don't just "get over" the loss of a child; they need to go through it, feeling every wave of emotion that comes along. This book validates the unique emotional experience of fathers and offers practical and compassionate guidance to navigate the grieving process.

As I've witnessed the growth of groups like Helping Fathers Heal, I am heartened to see more men finding the courage to step forward and seek understanding and support. This book provides a space for fathers to recognize their pain, understand it, and, most importantly, grow through it. *Helping Fathers Heal* is an essential read for any father navigating the tumultuous seas of grief. It's a book that gives men permission to grieve and empowers them to grow from their experiences.

- Brian D. Smith. Grief Guide, author of *Grief 2 Growth*, and host of Grief 2 Growth Podcast

§

Anyone who tells you "Time heals all wounds" has never lost a child.... I have.

This wonderful book is about grieving. But it's also about continuing to live after a loss. Sometimes a much different life, often one of service. And we cannot do that alone. We need to heal together. Thank you for sharing your heart. Albeit with a piece of it missing.

- Joe McQuillen is a father of three children. One on the other side. He is the author of *My Search for Christopher on the Other Side* and *We're Not Done Yet Pop; My Lessons from the Other Side* and a shining light parent.

§

Since the start of Helping Parents Heal, Inc. in 2009, our support group has been a safe place for parents and families to heal. However, the membership of moms has historically been proportionately much higher. It is easier for mothers to communicate the feelings they experience after the passing of one or more children, as well as the connection they feel with their children in the afterlife.

Dads heal differently. Therefore, it is essential to allow them to have a safe space to express themselves among like-minded souls. Mike Edwards created Helping Fathers Heal in February 2019. This healing affiliate, specifically for Fathers, has been an enormous help to many husbands and fathers searching for ways to move forward and heal.

Chris Ryan's beautiful new book, written exclusively by Dads from Helping Fathers Heal, will serve as a guidebook to healing for dads throughout the US and the world. We thank Mike, Chris, and the other dads for opening their hearts to this project and lifting the veil of silence. We are confident you will enjoy the heartwarming stories contained within and the remarkable personalities of the kids who inspired them.

- Elizabeth Boisson, President and Co-Founder, Helping Parents Heal, Inc.

Helping Fathers Heal

Grief, Hope, and our Search for Connection

Compiled and edited by Chris Ryan
Co-Edited by Tom Madsen

Foreword by Gordon Smith

Copyright © 2024 by Helping Parents Heal, Inc.
ISBN 9798876763563

Book Design by Chris Ryan & Reese Harris
Cover and layout by Reese Harris
Cover photo by Cyn Colip
Cover model: Sean Ryan

All rights reserved. No portion of this book, except for brief review, may be reproduced or transmitted in any form without written permission from Helping Parents Heal, Inc.

Table of Contents

Foreword i
Introduction iii
1 Taya's Dad, Harry B. 1
2 Lora's Dad, David S. 9
3 Sean's Dad, Chris R. 19
4 Peter's Dad, Martin S. 29
5 Ariel's Dad, Ish S. 37
6 Nolan's Dad, Warren G. 45
7 Christian's Dad, Roy S. 55
8 Devon's Dad, Jeff H. 63
9 Kyla's Dad, Jason W. 73
10 Ryan's Dad, Mike D. 79
11 Autumn's Dad, Mike J. 85
12 Zach's Dad, Jerry C. 95
13 Miles' Dad, David K. 105
14 Dylan's Dad, Mike E. 115
15 Austin's Dad, Jeff C. 123
16 Lexi's Dad, Matt G. 131
17 Matthew's Dad, Dan D. 139
18 Mike's Dad, Steven L. 145
19 Tyler's Dad, Will T. 153
20 Noah's Dad, Bunt T. 159
21 Kevin's Dad, Tom M. 165
22 Lauren's Dad, Tim H. 175
23 Zach's Dad, Chris D. 183
24 Jo's Dad, Jerry M. 189
25 Josh's Dad, Andy B. 197
Afterword 205
Acknowledgements 207

Helping Fathers Heal

Foreword
by Gordon Smith

I'm honored to offer these first words for this book because it contains a remarkable display of courage. Sharing our intimate emotions in a vulnerable way is not easy. And for men, it is even more challenging. Our society is grief-illiterate. Moreover, culturally, males are generally raised to refrain from showing emotion. Society teaches us to be strong and invulnerable, to maintain control, and to be a good example. To be strong and carry on. We aim to protect the ones we love. but sometimes we just cannot. These chapters are our reckoning.

These men share stories of grief and vulnerability and do it for a noble cause: seeking some form of help or healing from a wound that might never fully recover. These are stories of the devastating loss that comes with the passing of their child. And yet, they are also stories of hope. You will read about healthy healing through a connection with Spirit and other fathers. Helping Fathers Heal is a brotherhood in mourning that inspires and encourages its members when they falter. They pick each other up, and their grief is seen and heard. They are accepted, just as they are.

I've had the pleasure of meeting many of these fathers at the Helping Parents Heal Conference and during their weekly Zoom meetings. I've heard some of their stories and now you, too, will read and learn about their heartbreaking journeys and the full range of emotions that go with the various stages of grief. You'll hear dads who feel angry, guilty, and on a mission of justice. In my experience, Spirit has been working hard to allow these men to release their pain and sorrow. I've seen tremendous tenderness and love growing through the cracks of their broken hearts. I've seen heroic efforts to create foundations, hold blood drives, raise awareness about childhood diseases, or valiantly work to stop the imminent danger inherent in street drugs.

My entire adult life has been spent working to help people with loss. As a medium and light worker, I have encountered so much dark despairing sorrow, yet watch it turn to light and understanding that death from this world is not the end. These courageous fathers are the embodiment of that transformation of darkness into light. They have become light workers in their own right.

I hope that you find comfort and inspiration in these pages. I know from experience that healing occurs when people can share their hearts in a safe place with others who love and accept them. Helping Fathers Heal is a lovely example of that. May you hear the language of their hearts and absorb hope from their experiences. If it helps you, then it also helps the authors of these stories, for it gives purpose to their pain. And I'll tell you a little secret: their children are thrilled because they also want you to be comforted. Their message is, "You can't die for the life of you!"

With a career spanning over three decades, Gordon Smith has been hailed by the UK's media as "Britain's most accurate medium." Spiritual teacher, Public Speaker, and Author of 23 books to date, Gordon's accuracy has been tested at Glasgow University and published in three scientific journals.

Gordon Smith (far right) enjoys some time with other members of the Helping Fathers Heal Group at the 2022 HPH Conference. Photo courtesy of Rick Wilcoxson.

Introduction
by Chris Ryan

If you are holding this book, odds are you have experienced what is probably the most painful event imaginable: the passing of your own child. If that's true, I am very sorry...I can empathize. My son, Sean, transitioned from this earth in 2021 at the tender age of 23. My world crashed. I couldn't make sense of anything. How do I deal with this? What do I do next? I knew I had choices to make, but I couldn't see anything clearly. I felt empty inside and the world felt...different. Lonelier. I just couldn't understand: Why would this happen to me? What good could come from such a tragedy? What purpose did this loss of life, this sacrifice, serve?

We've found no blueprint for grieving. Every day is different and unpredictable. My wife and I no longer know what normal means and we are searching for any form of healing. This is usually a slow and painful process. We humans are programmed to learn from what happens to us in this life. With every event, we have a choice. We can choose to somehow adapt, or we can retreat. Succumbing to negative emotions such as fear can trigger a host of unhealthy reactions: isolation and loneliness, anger, and despair. As Darwin noted, survival requires us to adapt to an ever-evolving environment. But when you're dealing with the passing of one (or more) of your children, it can seem too much to handle.

Suffering the passing of your own child unleashes a tide of unique emotional conflicts for men because we have been conditioned to be the providers for, and protectors of, our families. The man is traditionally the one who provides security when there is danger. Times are changing, and some of these stereotypical roles are evolving. But the house many of us were raised in mirrored this familiar historical narrative; the man, the father, is supposed to be strong, physically and emotionally.

Our culture programs the male to control his emotions to maintain a stable and predictable façade. This can lead to a serious internal conflict when one is grieving a loss of this unimaginable magnitude. How can I take care of myself, express my emotions, and address my needs while also caring for my spouse or the other children? How do I compose myself and put on a brave face to function at work–and can I even think about working? Where do I go when I need to be real and vulnerable? Can I even BE vulnerable in such a crisis? Today's world sadly seems ever more desensitized to human sorrows. Unless someone has suffered the passing of a child themselves, they simply don't understand the devastating emotional toll it takes, and well-meaning people often steer clear of us on the grief journey. It takes courage to stand with a man who is suffering and in pain. Seeing a grown man break down in tears can make many people uncomfortable. In my quest for healing, I'm looking for support from people with the courage to be with me right here, right now...exactly how I am in this moment. I'm broken, I'm hurting, but I don't want to isolate myself and be alone. I need people I can feel "safe" with so I can drop any pretenses or inhibitions. This is a raw place, this grieving space we're in.

One of the first gut-wrenching tasks my wife and I had to face following our son Sean's passing was retrieving his belongings from the house where he rented a room. When we went to gather up his stuff, we received a sign from Sean. (You'll hear more about signs and synchronicities throughout this book.) The old house had an enclosed front porch that was typically littered with a variety of boxes, clothes, trash bags, and cigarette butts. The three young men who shared this rental were not tidy, to say the least. This porch is the spot where Sean was found by paramedics. However, when we went there a few days after the tragedy, the porch was curiously clean. We found an old couch, a spotless coffee table, and a clean ashtray. In that ashtray was a small, polished stone with one word engraved in gold. That word was "accept." We don't know how, or who put it there, but it hit me like a ton of bricks. After having been in Al-Anon groups for several years, I knew the idea of acceptance was the first of the 12 steps to recovery. This stone was one of a multitude of signs we've received that have helped us along the path of healing.

After Sean transitioned, my wife, Cyn, dove into research, reading books on spirituality and the afterlife. Little did we know there was so much new data and progress in the area of consciousness that transcends death. Online searches turned up a number of resources, one of which was a nonprofit support group called Helping Parents Heal. You will read about it multiple times in this book. Cyn joined their Facebook group and attended several meetings on Zoom, where parents shared stories about signs sent by their children and discussed ways to feel closer to that departed loved one. Many had been comforted by "connections" made with the help of mediums. Some had even been able to tune their consciousness and contact their children in Spirit. These progressive ideas aligned with our own beliefs: a part of us doesn't die when the body does. Our soul (or whatever word you wish to use) lives on. Sean lives on! We attended the Helping Parents Heal conference in Phoenix and were stunned at the positive energy and hope that pervaded the ballroom of 900+ attendees.

At this conference, there was a breakout session of dads who met weekly via Zoom, a group called "Helping Fathers Heal." In this room and throughout that weekend, I began to see that these grieving dads had created a safe place to be real, be vulnerable, be honest, and be able to vent emotions, father-to-father. "I'm not alone," I told my wife.

This book is written by some of the men in the Helping Fathers Heal support group. They are courageous souls from points around the world who are willing to be fully present in each other's pain. If one dad is struggling, there are others available to pick him up with support and encouragement. Of course, grief doesn't magically vanish. We will never be the same men we were before our children passed, but we can experience a form of healing. Our group does this by sharing our journey, being open and honest, and witnessing each other's grief. Community is a key ingredient to helping heal your heart and find a way forward despite the grief. As one father said, "Grieving is a team sport."

As you read the chapters, you'll hear these dads' stories in unfiltered voices. We gave each writer ten questions to help them compose their essay. We wanted them to share about themselves and their child, tell us what happened, and what they've learned on their journey to try to deal with their grief. We only edited for brevity, clarity, and grammar. Please give us some grace as our stories unfold. You'll see us refer to our child in both the present and past tense...intentionally. Each dad has a unique writing style. We are not experienced writers; we're a collection of men who wake up, perhaps go to work, or otherwise attempt to lead a "normal" life. The exercise of writing about our loss and suffering doesn't come second nature. In fact, it was quite a difficult assignment for all of us as we opened our emotional wounds to re-live an episode that broke our hearts wide open.

We hope that you will find a form of community here. We encourage you to find your own tribe of support on this journey. If you are a dad, perhaps you will want to join one of our Helping Fathers Heal meetings. We would welcome the chance to meet you and hear your child's story. We try our best to celebrate their life as we remember and honor them, grateful for the contribution these advanced souls made to us personally, and to others in their orbit. As fathers experiencing grief, we seek to get comfortable with the UNcomfortable and stretch ourselves spiritually. We listen, and we stand in the fire with our brothers. We hope you will discover tools to help soothe your pain in this time of profound sorrow. Most of all, we seek to offer glimpses of the hope we have found on this journey. It's this hope that inspires us to keep going, and to honor–even celebrate–our children by living a life of purpose.

"Life shrinks or expands in proportion to one's courage."
- Anais Nin

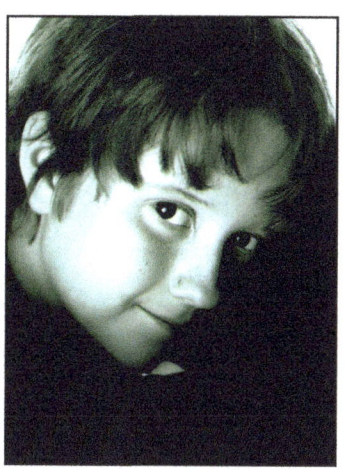

*Dedicated to Sean Gabriel Ryan, our only child on earth,
our angel in Spirit, our teacher, and our inspiration for this collection.*

1 Taya's Dad, Harry B.

The alarm went off at 5:23 a.m. on February 2, 2016, and although it would be a few minutes before we realized it, the nightmare that would engulf us had occurred five hours earlier. It had snowed all night, piling up over 18 inches deep. My wife, Jenny, and I had both slept well, perhaps comforted by that blanket of snow covering our home. After rubbing the sleep from my eyes, I read an overnight text alerting us that school was canceled due to the storm, a rare occurrence that would make both kids happy.

I then saw an email that our 14-year-old daughter, Taya, sent us at 11:36 p.m. the night before with a blank subject line. It simply read, "I love you." My first reaction was a warm feeling that maybe she finally accepted that we did love her. Taya had been convinced that we hated her, typical of some people who live with Borderline Personality Disorder (BPD). I showed the email to Jenny. We both realized, at the same moment, that it might instead be a sign of something horrible. Jenny took our dog downstairs to let him out while I went to check on Taya. I didn't really think she had done anything, but I had to know.

I walked down the hallway and then up the seven steps to Taya's bedroom. I opened her door, and everything looked normal. The shades were pulled tightly across her balcony door, as they were day and night. The decorative lights she had recently made using Christmas lights and a box of cupcake holders were still on, illuminating the space under the loft bed she and I had built together during spring break the year before. The ladder to the loft bed was on the right just inside the doorway, and I climbed up to give Taya the good news about the snow day, and to alleviate our fears that something was wrong. I poked my head over the railing to find an empty bed. A tidal wave of panic swept through me. Where was she at 5:30 in the morning? I looked to the left, scanning the room, and saw her hanging in the place where her swing was supposed to be. I screamed a noise that Jenny later said she had never heard before, a primal scream of complete horror and despair, as if my heart were being ripped out of me alive.

To the outside world, Taya was a superstar. At age 14, she was a junior in high school (two grades ahead) and taking calculus at the University of Colorado. Her high school selected her as one of three students to participate in a district-wide leadership program. She co-founded the writing club, co-chaired the Environmental Task Force, and was featured on the PBS Newshour about volunteering to teach senior citizens how to use computers. She had a beloved best friend. Taya was beautiful, charismatic, and fun. But she wasn't happy, and it wasn't just depression. She had a fear of abandonment that alternated between extremes of idealization and devaluation in her close relationships. She had an unstable sense of her own identity, often felt empty, had trouble controlling her anger, had dissociative feelings, and—a year and a half earlier—had started an escalating pattern of self-harming behavior. After

1 Taya's Dad, Harry B.

she passed, we found her writings including this description of how she often felt:

> You don't know what it's like, to be bursting like a river inside, so much inside of you and nowhere for it to go. A sea of thoughts and emotions caught, trapped inside your body so your very skin starts to explode. Pores erupting because no one understands, no one cares. No way to escape or get out because it's all you, creating and filling and stretching your body with feelings. Every day is another straw on the already broken back—you're just waiting for it to fall apart and disintegrate. The waves rock inside and push and pull and there's no way to escape, no solace from this never-ending nightmare. Everything hurts, just need to be alone and stay alone. Can't be around anybody who will kill yourself or your body or you, not you but what makes you you. Everybody and everything hurts like salt on a freshly cut wound. A rocket shooting off into space and then being stopped and turned around, because it has no energy left. A spool of golden thread which keeps unraveling and unraveling until there's nothing left, just an empty roll of cardboard which is tossed away.

We didn't know everything going on, but we knew Taya was struggling. Four months before she transitioned, we hospitalized Taya after we found suicide notes on her bed. The hospital released her saying that she was not suicidal. I consulted with a counselor at her school who thought Taya might have a personality disorder. My wife, my son, and I independently looked at the criteria for the various personality disorders and we each pinpointed BPD as a clear description of Taya's behavior. The experts we later consulted, along with the writings, social media posts, blogs, and texts we found after she transitioned, reinforced our belief that she had BPD.

Anywhere from 2% to 6% of the general public live with BPD and 10% of those with BPD pass by suicide. Ninety percent of people with BPD attempt suicide and the average person with BPD has more than three lifetime attempts. Even though the medical literature and diagnostic manuals clearly state that BPD can begin in adolescence (or earlier), many mental health professionals refuse to diagnose BPD until the individual is at least 18 years old. This is based on a fear that the symptoms of BPD might be confused with adolescence, or that it would stigmatize the person. When we brought the concept of BPD to Taya's therapist, she dismissed it out of hand. Similarly, a few months later, her psychiatrist said that he would consider a BPD diagnosis only if the symptoms persisted after she turned 18. This made no sense to me; how can the mental health system effectively treat children with this serious mental illness if so many professionals refuse to diagnose them? Borderline Personality Disorder killed Taya before she was old enough for misguided professionals to provide the diagnosis and treatment that may well have saved her life. As I learned more, this injustice fueled my grieving by providing a new mission to keep other young people from suffering as Taya did. First, though, our family had to grapple with the immediate pain of losing her.

In the weeks after Taya's passing, I fell into the role of the supporter for my wife and 16-year-old son. I walked with Jenny to the bus stop each morning for her commuter bus to Denver and then met her bus in the evening. Our son had started college the year before and I walked with him the mile to his morning classes and then walked back to meet him after class. If he had an afternoon class, I repeated the circuit, walking several miles each day. I worked from home so I could flex my schedule, often making phone calls on my return walks after dropping him off. Our son and I talked about Taya on each walk, the years of her deteriorating mental illness, and its impact on her and the family. I did all the cooking and laundry, often while on conference calls in the pre-Zoom days. I delayed my own grieving, focusing instead on supporting others.

In those early weeks and months, I also dove deeply into the "why" question, especially related to BPD. With support from Google and the Boulder Police Department, I obtained a download of Taya's phone and accessed her Google Drive with thousands of documents and email messages. I found four blogs she had written under pseudonyms, thousands of downloaded photos, and multiple social media profiles. With increasing horror, I saw the mental trauma she suffered and the deterioration of her rational brain activity.

1 Taya's Dad, Harry B.

Most frustratingly, I found times when she had reached out on her own to professionals who then dismissed her. I became determined to support other young people with BPD by sharing Taya's story as a case study showing that young people can indeed have BPD and should be treated for it. Over the next four years, I meticulously researched Taya's decline and then wrote and published, *TAYA: A Case for the Diagnosis of Borderline Personality Disorder in Children*. Working on and writing the book provided a focus and outlet for my grief while also—selfishly—keeping me close to Taya by diving into her world. The book also connected me to the BPD world when two national experts agreed to write the foreword and afterword of the book. I've been fortunate to join the Board of Directors of several organizations focused on BPD or mental health. I testified on a pair of bills in California this year that will help address these issues. Advocacy is what worked for me. Other dads on this journey have re-focused on their self-care, engaged more deeply with their families, or delved into a variety of other outlets. No single pathway is better than another. It's what works for you.

Taya passed in what we had always thought would be our forever home. Although we had only lived there for 16 months, we loved the home for its quirky design, location at the base of the mountains, and room for lots of visitors. Almost immediately after Taya passed over, Jenny and our son wanted to move. I wasn't ready and they consented to stay until I was, which took another year. During that year, I realized that I no longer had a passion for my work with conservation corps, the field that had consumed me for the previous quarter century. My professional interests, like so much else, all changed on one dreary snowy day in February.

Subsequently, I became focused on the mental health field and—in particular—on young people with BPD. After searching for months, I was fortunate to be hired to run PathPoint, a nonprofit organization in California that supports people with mental health disorders and/or developmental disabilities. Jenny and I moved to Santa Barbara, close to where we have family. At PathPoint, I feel a deep emotional connection to the individuals we support and their families. Every day I feel that I am making a difference, and I strive to do so with kindness, compassion, and humility.

Focusing on supporting my family, writing the book, and jumping headfirst into a new job allowed me to delay much of my grieving and, unsurprisingly, it caught up to me a few years after the move. I fell into a depression that I couldn't pull myself out of. We had taken part, as a couple, in two support groups in Colorado and had undergone EMDR (Eye Movement Desensitization and Reprocessing) sessions for the traumatic moment of finding Taya. I also participated in the online support group, *Parents of Suicide*. None of this could pull me out of my funk. Friends helped me find a local male therapist who, over several months, helped me address the guilt that was eating me from the inside like an unwanted parasite hollowing out my core. Regardless of any professional accomplishments, I felt like a complete failure for being unable to support my daughter to reach adulthood, my most important job on this planet. Consequently, I felt unworthy of receiving love or even being alive. The therapist helped me understand the importance of balancing the emotional and rational sides of my brain while also confirming my natural feelings of guilt. With his support, and the love of my wife and son, I pulled through. I still have these guilt feelings, though now they mostly live in the background where I can balance them with rational thoughts.

I wish that I had found Helping Parents Heal—and in particular, Helping Fathers Heal—much sooner than I did. Participating in an all-male support group has been transformative; I realized that I often unconsciously play a "protector" or "supporter" role in groups with both women and men. In the all-male HFH group, I am more able to focus on my own support needs.

Jenny and I had a strong relationship before we lost Taya. I'm sure that was instrumental in us emerging even stronger together after her transition. What worked most was respecting that we were each grieving differently and that was okay. Seven years after losing Taya, we co-wrote the book, *The After Journey: A Survivor's Guide After the Passing of a Loved One by Suicide*. The process of writing together brought us even closer. In addition to being best friends and lovers, we feel like a formidable team and that feels good.

I never believed in the afterlife or any connections to people who

1 Taya's Dad, Harry B.

had passed. I suffered a devastating loss when I was 24 years old; my fiancée developed non-Hodgkin's lymphoma and passed four months later. I didn't see signs, or even look for signs from her, and I had no belief that she continued to exist in any form. Several months after Taya passed, a friend connected us with a local medium. Jenny met with him a few times informally and one time, while she was talking with him on the phone, he asked to speak with me. I was skeptical when I took the phone from Jenny. He first spoke about Taya, sharing information that was meaningful, but not necessarily convincing to a skeptic. He then said that he had someone else who wanted to talk with me, my wife who had a name beginning with an R. I was shocked as he then told me four things about Rosie, my fiancée who passed, that I had never told anyone else. When I handed the phone back to Jenny, my worldview had been radically altered in a way I never expected.

Over the following months, I heard both Taya and Rosie in my thoughts and began seeing signs. Four years after Taya passed, I had a dream of a dead dolphin that had washed up on the beach. In my dream, I asked how the dolphin died and Taya, in her characteristic dark humor, playfully answered that perhaps it hung itself. We live two blocks from the beach and we're on it almost every day, though I had never seen a dead dolphin there. On February 2nd—Taya's Angelversary—Jenny and I took a long walk on the beach. On our way back, retracing the part of the beach we had walked 30 minutes earlier, we came across a large dead dolphin that had just washed up. On March 7th—Taya's birthday—we took another long walk on the beach and came across two scientists sitting below some rocks. We came closer and saw that they were examining another dead dolphin that had washed up. We've walked this section of beach hundreds of times in the years since those two special days and have yet to see another dead dolphin.

I know that Taya is out there, somewhere. I know there is more than we can ever understand. I know that there will be much more to discover someday. I know that the definition of "human" is not what I once thought, and that "birth" and "death" have new meanings. I close with this short piece that Taya wrote, which shows that perhaps she understood more of this unconsciously than we ever knew...

I am human.

And I can fly. I can float up upon the thoughts of a purring kitten, lift myself past the barriers. I can learn, write, fill my small mortal body with thoughts and ideas and emotions so intense that they physically affect me. I can understand myself, and the people around me. I can say what I think, even if it isn't the right thing to say. I have a voice, an opinion, a life. I have myself, and no one will ever take that away from me.

I am human, and I am unstoppable.

2 Lora's Dad, David S.

Lora Ann Schansberg is the youngest of my five children. As a youth, Lora was very energetic with an infectious smile and unforgettable laugh. Lora's tight blond curls were the perfect match for her ever-present smile. As the youngest of five, she was spoiled accordingly and took full advantage. Her primary passions were sports, soccer, singing, and ceramics. She was a very competitive person and started for her high school varsity soccer team as a freshman and sophomore, hoping to follow two of her sisters by playing college soccer.

At age 17, I took her to the local urgent care facility for fatigue, following her fall club soccer season. The doctor was concerned about her lab results and sent us directly to the local hospital for further blood work. She was diagnosed with Polycythemia Vera, a very rare blood cancer. The next day, Lora was admitted to the pediatric hematology and oncology ward at the University of Wisconsin (UW) Children's Hospital. She went through a couple of weeks of tests and treatments to confirm the initial diagnosis. Her lead UW hematologist referred us to the Mayo Clinic, as Polycythemia Vera is virtually unheard of in somebody that young. While at UW, I spent most of my time reading about the disease to better understand what my baby was facing. The internet and a sick child are a dangerous combination. I knew from my research it was very serious. The Mayo specialist confirmed my greatest fear. Lora indeed had this rare, terminal form of blood cancer.

That day at Mayo began my family's arduous journey through hell. It was the first time any doctor actually used the word "cancer." For twelve years we watched our precious Lora weaken a little bit each day. There were hundreds of doctors' appointments, procedures, surgeries, chemo, experimental drugs, and lengthy hospital stays. When I wasn't by Lora's side, I was advocating for her with her team of hematologists, oncologists, cardiologists, neurologists, and pulmonologists, and wading through an endless flood of insurance paperwork. I fought for 18 months with the State of Wisconsin so Lora could receive disability insurance to help with the mountain of hospital bills and ridiculous drug costs.

Lora's highly competitive nature and perseverance served her well during this struggle. I admired her courage and her will to fight. She taught me what real strength is. Lora's mom often stayed with her during the frequent hospital stays. I was still working, so I usually commuted to and from the hospital. That hour-long drive was my time to contemplate, cry and release.

Lora and I had a very strong relationship. She was my baby! After Lora's mom and I divorced when she was 11, Lora lived with me. We spent an inordinate amount of windshield time together traveling to sporting events and, after diagnosis, on our weekly 60-mile trips to UW and occasional trips to Mayo. We talked endlessly on those trips. I tried to always be the positive, optimistic, and supportive dad for her, but Lora saw through that smoke screen with her brutal honesty and dark sense of humor. Lora's favorite thing was road trips. We took many trips together until her health declined to the point that travel became too difficult. Our favorite road trip was to our cabin in Northern Wisconsin. She fell in love with the sights, sounds and smells of nature. The lake house became her safe haven and escape. One of my favorite memories was sitting on the screened-in porch during a rainstorm listening to all the different sounds the rain made hitting different surfaces. We tried to take at least one significant trip each year. Our favorites were her Make-A-Wish trip to Hawaii with her mom and brother, a birthday week in Door County, an adventure traveling up the Lake Michigan coast, and exploring Italy for two weeks. I barely survived the Italy trip. Pushing her wheelchair over the cobblestones of Ancient Rome brought back bad memories of the blocking sleds in high school football. All our trips were filled with laughter and fun, a very welcome diversion from the stark realities of her disease. But the trips also provided us with the time to discuss end of life, after-life, and funerals. As difficult as it is to watch your child's physical and mental health slowly and steadily deteriorate, I also feel like I developed a closeness with Lora that exceeded the close relationships I had with my four older children. In a way, I am very thankful for that. I retired from my job early so I could spend as much time with my daughter as possible. The stress made full concentration at work next to impossible.

As Lora's health declined to the point that all medical measures had been exhausted, her medical team directed us to hospice. The complexities of home care had become overwhelming. Lora was admitted to an in-facility hospice center for end-of-life care and pain management in November of 2020. Every day seemed like a damn vigil, but we filled those days playing games, listening to music, and watching Lora's favorite shows. To the doctors' surprise, Lora made it to Thanksgiving, which we celebrated at hospice. Then, we celebrated her nephew's and niece's mid-December birthdays at the facility. We decorated her room for Christmas, and we were all surprised and thankful we were able to celebrate one final Christmas together...Lora's favorite holiday.

One night, in a lucid moment, Lora said my dad was visiting her in her dreams and waiting to meet her. She never knew my dad, as he had transitioned the year before she was born. Then she asked me, "Who is Ruby?" My jaw dropped. Ruby was my aunt who passed away when I was 8 years old. I barely have any memories of her, and I don't recall ever mentioning her to Lora. My other kids had no recollection of me ever talking about my Aunt Ruby. Lora said Ruby was with my dad and "many other beautiful people." I recalled being with my own mother when she transitioned, and just before her final breath she smiled and said, "Hi, Mom." Pretty chilling stuff for this skeptic.

Right after Christmas Lora began drifting in and out of consciousness. The heavy pain meds made her pretty much incoherent. New Year's Eve arrived, and Lora's siblings came as we knew her transition was near. We all took turns embracing her, holding her hand, and whispering in her ear. Pele, her dog and constant companion, was curled up by her feet. Her mother was cuddling her. I was stroking her hair and holding her hand. I whispered to Lora how much I loved her, how thankful I was that she was my daughter, and how much I admired and respected her unrelenting fight against this hideous disease. I told her to go find my dad. I refused to tell her goodbye because I knew in my heart that she would always be with me. I did ask her to always surround me with her beautiful energy.

At 10:00 p.m. on New Year's Eve she drew her final breath.

Her pain was over.

Mine had just begun.

I had rehearsed this moment countless times in my mind. I thought I might experience some sense of relief because the previous 12 years of Lora's life had been hell for our family. I was wrong. Witnessing her demise over the last six months was brutal. But the devastation of losing my youngest child was an immediate new level of pain. I was lost in a fog of shock, sadness, frustration, and uncertainty. I had no motivation to do anything. I didn't want to go anywhere or see anyone. I felt like I lost part of my identity as a father and as a person.

Lora's mom and I became closer because we felt we were the only people who could truly understand. Lora's siblings all reacted differently and grieved in their own ways. Some were quiet and withdrawn. Others needed to vent and talk. They all went through the stages of grief at different times and in different ways. This helped me understand that everybody grieves differently and there is clearly no blueprint for this process. I could not tell them how to grieve. I didn't know how! I could only offer to be there for them. Everybody needs to navigate these dark and choppy waters their own way. Your path is unique.

Some of the most helpful guidance I received was prior to Lora's transition. Hospice helps the family prepare and deal with the inevitable grief. We had a family counseling session with the hospice grief support team the week before Lora went into hospice. I listened while my family expressed their thoughts and fears. I believed I had suppressed my emotions well enough to avoid participating in this "interrogation." Then one of the counselors who was sitting to my left put her hand on my arm, looked me straight in the eye and said, "Lora is most concerned about you and how you will handle this." Shit. Lora had exposed my tough guy shtick in her prior meeting with the team. They had saved me for last.

I was asked what I was feeling about Lora facing end-of-life care.

Easy. Intense anger. I was pissed at the world. I was beyond angry that my daughter was being ripped away from me at age 29 and nobody, especially me, could do a damn thing about it. As a man, I like to control shit, especially when it comes to protecting my precious family. I have never played the helpless victim well. I am wired to solve problems and make things happen. And, like many guys, I don't want to talk about it.

The counselor explained that anger is a very intense emotion that easily rises to the forefront during difficult situations, often masking true causes of the anger. Next, the counselor asked, "Why are you angry?"

"Duh...my youngest daughter is dying!"

The counselor replied, "Of course, but try to understand what is causing your anger because you can work on those reasons." I thought for a few moments and realized I was angry because I was extremely sad and scared to lose my daughter. They challenged me to express my sadness and fear in constructive ways rather than internalizing the emotions.

Someone tipped off the counselors that I loved to draw and write. (Lora was always a master manipulator.) The counselors challenged me to express my feelings and thoughts through those creative outlets. I wrote a 24-page poem to Lora expressing the feelings I could not verbalize. I shared it with her before she passed. I created a 30-minute video for the family of all my favorite Lora pictures set to her favorite music. We watched it together in hospice with a few of her closest friends. Using creative channels was very helpful and enabled me to work through some of the anger.

I didn't know which way was up for several months. Everything was surreal. Three months after Lora transitioned, my family wanted to honor her by raising funds for Agrace Hospice, which was outstanding in Lora's end-of-life care. We shared Lora's story with the community and reached out to friends, co-workers, Lora's teammates, and local businesses. The response was overwhelming. We raised over $100,000 in Lora's memory so other families could experience the wonderful and compassionate level of care we received.

Agrace asked for input as to where to channel the money and we chose nursing scholarships. Lora had planned to study nursing in college. Today, some of Lora's Certified Nursing Assistants have finished or will soon finish nursing school. Other nurses are furthering their education and training with the scholarship money we raised.

Our community showed support in other ways. Lora's soccer club planted a tree with a plaque at the soccer complex in her honor. The club also set up an annual sportsmanship award in her name. I had coached Lora for 12 years. There is now a special bench and plaque installed midfield on the high school soccer field. This was done in Lora's honor by several of her soccer teammates. Such events are emotionally difficult, but highly rewarding. Knowing your child will never be forgotten is heartwarming.

The first two years of the grieving process were tough. I withdrew from friends, activities, and any social gatherings. I felt like I was just treading water to stay alive. I slept poorly. I drank more. I did not take my own health seriously. The first year was a smothering fog. The second year was actually tougher for me psychologically and emotionally. I started having happy moments again but felt guilty for being happy. The second year was more terrifying because you begin to see more clearly. Reality sets in.

The grief journey is very personal, a roller coaster of emotions. Triggers seemingly come out of nowhere. I am unexpectedly blindsided by tearful moments of unbearable loss. There are days I simply can't function, so I don't. Rather than question what is wrong with me or why am I like this, I am coming to accept there will be very bad days to just ride out. There is nothing wrong with me. I lost my child! I have earned the right to be sad sometimes.

I get so much from our Helping Fathers Heal group. This group of loving dads understands. They walk in my shoes. While our circumstances and situations may be quite different, we all share the pain of unimaginable loss. From experience comes wisdom, and with wisdom comes understanding. With better understanding comes healing, in time. Wisdom is shared every day in the HFH group.

Some of the great advice I have taken from HFH includes:
- Be kind to yourself!
- When it comes to grief, be patient because healing takes time.
- Your life has been shattered into a million pieces, and as you begin putting those pieces together, accept that some of those pieces are missing and you have to rebuild your life with what is left.

Losing my daughter has taught me how fragile and precious life is. On the other hand, I no longer fear death because I understand there is more after this life. If I am struggling, I give myself the space and time to work through it. There will be good days ahead and I accept there will always be bad days, too. For the first two-plus years the many memories I have of my sweet child used to make me sad. Now, as I try to move forward in my journey, I find those memories to be heartwarming reminders of wonderful moments of life to be cherished, not missed. When we share special family moments, I always share a thought or story about Lora so she will continue to be part of future memories.

Grief has also taught me:
- I am stronger than I thought, but I am weaker than I care to admit.
- I am more willing to share feelings, but if I feel like bottling it up, that's ok, too.
- You must do you when it comes to grief.
- I hate being sad, but I accept some days will be. I cry when I need to.

My outlook on family has shifted. I am less concerned with money and "stuff" and more focused on making lasting memories through shared experiences. I try to be there for my kids and grandkids more often. And I really enjoy sharing unexpected surprises with them.

I feel my daughter's energy all around me. Lora visits me in three primary ways:
1. I get signs. The signs I most often associate with Lora are deer, cardinals, eagles, and white butterflies. I see those weekly. Lora and I have a shared love for wildlife.
2. She continues to prank me. Lora always found great humor and joy in my mishaps. She proudly pranked friends and family. I use a walker to help with my bad knees. One time, I loaded up my walker with six 12-packs of soda. I turned to close the trunk and when I turned back, I saw my walker rolling down the driveway and out into the middle of the road. Her laughter was echoing in my head. In another instance, I was driving to Madison to watch a grandson play baseball. On our many trips to and from UW hospital, Lora and I would argue which shortcut was the fastest. I was fondly thinking about this when I drove past her shortcut. When I turned the corner onto my preferred route, a gallon jug of distilled water flew off the front seat and landed between my feet, preventing me from using the brake and gas pedals.

3. Dream visits. Every couple of months, I get a very vivid dream visitation. They are so real, full of vibrant colors, with smells, sounds and the feeling of touch. In the most recent visitation Lora was about four years old. She was sitting in the back of my truck waiting for me. She had her arms extended and was wiggling her fingers saying, "Daddy, I love you. Gimme a hug." I grabbed her and held her tight. I could feel her heartbeat during the embrace. I could smell her hair. I felt her kiss on my cheek. It was wonderful. The next morning, I looked at Facebook and it had posted 12 Memories from Lora about our road-trip to Michigan.

Are signs real? They are for me. They make me feel great, and when I am battling my grief, I will take any moments of solace and happiness I can get. You have to open your heart to the possibility of noticing the signs. I am uplifted by the other dads in HFH when they share their stories about signs.

Lora's mom has found great comfort in medium readings. She feels they help her connect with Lora in a deeper way and provide validation of the afterlife. I was not a big believer in mediums initially, but I had an amazing reading with Kat Baillie. I really believe Lora was communicating with me through Kat....once my parents stopped interrupting to say hello.

I recently committed myself to three things that have really helped me find more peace and comfort:

First, I attend as many of my grandson's baseball games as I can. My oldest grandson played in college and this summer his American Legion team won State and went to National Regionals. My younger grandson won State, National Regionals and played in the Babe Ruth World Series. I would have deeply regretted missing any of it. I like to think Lora had a hand in getting me off my ass and going to so many of the games. It was a stark reminder for me to enjoy what is possible today rather than dwelling on the past.

Secondly, I started drawing again. I haven't drawn much since college. Lora was my inspiration and the subject matter for many drawings. We shared a love for the creative arts. I had forgotten how much enjoyment drawing brought to my life. I am more at peace and relaxed when I am creating.

Thirdly, I keep expanding and improving Lora's Memorial Garden. After

Lora transitioned, I began converting the backyard into a private butterfly garden and salsa garden in Lora's honor. Every year, our family adds to it. Everyone has had a hand in it; planting, weeding, harvesting, and eating the veggies.

Almost three years into this journey, and I have found it helpful to stay busier and engage in activities that I truly enjoy. It sounds simple, but it is harder than you think. Find your passions and embrace them.

The best advice I can offer is:
Broken crayons can still color, so color!
Do what you love because enjoyment helps ease pain.
Accept that there will be some crappy days.
Lean on those you trust and open your heart.... vulnerability is not a negative. Helping Fathers Heal has been, and is, great for this.

The bottom line is you survived the shittiest, most catastrophic hell any parent can experience...give yourself some credit for being a strong survivor. I hope you find happiness. You deserve it.

Peace and love, brothers!

3 Sean's Dad, Chris R.

As I write this, I'm only two years into my grief journey. So far, it's been an uneven road full of ups and downs. Most will tell you, healing is not a "straight line." As a dad, I miss my boy so very much it literally hurts my heart. Sometimes it feels like a massive weight on my chest. There are unpredictable rolling waves of emotions. It can be a very lonely experience, this grief.

Sean was our one and only. We tried to get pregnant for many years and even endured a miscarriage in the process. During the pregnancy, we settled on the name Gabriel. In part, because it was the Angel Gabriel who announced two miraculous births in the Bible. This name was perfect, as we thought of our baby as a miracle from heaven. Closing in on 40 years old, we had almost given up hope of getting pregnant. We ultimately chose Sean as a first name, in honor of his Godmother, and Gabriel became a middle name. We often referred to Sean as our "Angel Boy."

I find it curious how a child comes into our lives as this angelic, peaceful little being full of innocence and joy. As parents, we radiate pride and hope and envision dreams for the future. The baby quickly evolves into a child with a personality, and with talents and emotions that seem baked in. Sean was no different. He displayed an independent spirit at a young age. He acted as if we were all equals, like a three-legged stool. He didn't do as he was told simply because we were his parents. It had to make sense to him first, so there was a lot of explanation and persuasion involved when it came to his upbringing. To call him stubborn would be accurate, but it sometimes served him well. One of my favorite memories is when he was a Little League pitcher. Not many of his 10 and 11-year-old teammates could throw the ball over the plate. At this age, there are lots of balls and plenty of swings and misses. But Sean had an arm and steely confidence to go to the mound and get the job done. In one memorable game, his team was up by one run in the last inning. The opposing team had the bases loaded with one out. Our pitcher just wasn't getting the ball over the plate. They pulled him from the mound and put Sean in. Eight throws later and the inning–and game–were over! Sean's teammates jumped all over him, but he was very matter-of-fact about it all. No arrogance. It's just what you do. That was one of those "proud dad" moments.

Throughout his life, Sean was passionate about music, like his dad. I'd worked on the air in radio for 20 years and constantly played music in the house and car. When Sean was 11, we gave him an electric guitar and he taught himself to play. Thanks to YouTube and the use of "tabs" he was able to learn many of his favorite songs.

As he matured, Sean began watching videos and listening to interviews with his musical heroes. Before long he was hearing about the drugs and alcohol that often accompany the lifestyle. He began talking to me about what these musicians were taking and asking if I had ever done the same.

"Did you ever smoke pot, Dad?"

"Did you ever take LSD?"

This is a tough one for many parents. I didn't want to feed his curiosity and legitimize the use of illegal substances, especially at his age and because of the potency and dangers of present-day street drugs. So, I said, "Yeah, I tried pot, but it didn't work for me...I didn't really like it." That's true for me today.

Sean continued to research music, musicians, and their various methods of inspiration. Then, the difficult middle school years...and the introduction of many new friends. Some good kids, but some were pushing the edge. A few of his friends were experimenting with pot. Sean had done his research, and decided to experiment with pot as well. It didn't matter what we said or how we tried to deter him. He ran his own life and kept secrets. Along with the smoking, he started to drink with his friends. His mom and I were trying to be good parents and we tried our best to coach Sean and guide his decisions. "He's doing what we did...experiment. He'll grow out of it," we told ourselves. When he got in trouble at school, we didn't helicopter in to defend or save him. We let him be held accountable. It was a constant dance between freedom and restrictions.

Sean and I went to a lot of concerts when he was too young to drive himself. He and his best friend, Luke, would ask us dads to take them to see bands like The Flaming Lips, Grizzly Bear, and Linkin Park. The music was great, and it was good bonding time for us. Those are some of my favorite memories from Sean's teenage years. But Sean was keenly aware of the kids in the crowd who were getting high. His curiosity only grew.

In early high school the drug experimentation continued, and his grades plummeted. Household chores weren't getting done. He started sneaking out of the house and spending the night "out" with friends. He had very little academic ambition and his attitude went somewhat dark. We noticed it in his clothing, as well as, his demeanor. Once again, we tried to keep a respectful distance as parents while, also, keeping an eye on him. Raising a headstrong kid had its challenges.

Ultimately, things did not improve and by Sean's junior year of high school we had had enough. We saw family and substance abuse counselors for help. Ultimately, we sent him off to Utah for six weeks of therapeutic Wilderness Camping. (There are many such camps and companies, ours was not a "bootcamp" experience). It felt like a desperate attempt to save his life.

In the end, it didn't keep him from his self-destructive path.

This was followed by six difficult years of alcohol abuse, heavy drug use (mostly Xanax), and the intervention/rehab/sober living/back home merry-go-round. Eventually, when Sean was 21, we asked him to move out of the house and find other living arrangements . We wanted desperately to help, but also needed to maintain our own sanity. It was heartbreaking to live with someone you dearly love, but whose choices are causing such chaos. Sean's life seemed to be unraveling in front of our eyes and we were helpless to control his situation. In Al Anon, we learned about the "Three C's of addiction: We didn't Cause it, we can't Control it, and we can't Cure it."

On Saturday, September 4, 2021, we got The Call. "Can you come to the Emergency Room; your son is very sick." Sean had been resuscitated after his heart had stopped. No one knew how long his brain had been without oxygen, but at that moment, the doctor on the other end of the line said Sean wasn't responsive. There was no brainwave activity. I dropped the phone as my heart sank and I slumped to the floor and began sobbing. There was a heavy feeling in my chest and sickness in the pit of my stomach. Going to the hospital scared me, as I envisioned seeing him hooked up to machines; unable to see us; unable to smile.

The next two days in the ICU were a blur. Sean's body needed more and more life-supporting medications to keep him alive. His organs were failing. It was time to make a very difficult decision. The doctor said he would somehow get my wife back in the room despite the COVID protocol limiting the visitors to just one at a time. Cyn rejoined me, and we made the most consequential, brutally awful decision of our lives: to remove Sean from life support. We sat by his bed as they disconnected his I.V., respirator, dialysis, and monitoring devices. They gave him one final dose of morphine to ensure he was peaceful as his body slowly shut down. We were witnessing our only child slip away. Cyn was holding his hand, and I was on the other side of the bed with my hand on his chest. Within 10 minutes, his breathing slowed, and his heartbeat grew faint. The final monitor hooked up to his pulse showed a flatline. Cyn cried, "he's gone." He was two weeks shy of his 24th birthday. September has become a difficult month of anniversaries and painful memories.

We knew he had been self-medicating for years to alleviate his anxiety and depression. He thought he had purchased Ketamine through an online source. The death certificate said otherwise. He had a fatal combination of Xanax and fentanyl in his system.

Thus began our journey into grief. We were once again a childless couple. All our dreams for Sean to get married, settle into adulthood, bring grandchildren into the world, and watch us as we grew old had faltered... ALL of these dreams came crashing down around us.

The world suddenly felt empty to me. Everything was quite surreal. Nothing mattered; certainly not the tremendous amount of work I had lined up that month. My "old" life seemed abstract and distant; like it was now someone else's life. Deadlines became irrelevant. I went back and forth between what to do next logistically with Sean's body, and how to function in the world.

Cyn and I were both in a strange type of "survival" mode which allowed us to put one foot in front of the other. We walked from the hospital to a nearby restaurant where we could sit outside and away from others. We weren't hungry, but we were functioning on adrenaline and emotion. The sun was going down and the clouds began to turn golden. That's when I saw my first sign. I said to Cyn, "Look at those clouds!" Without another word, she saw it, too. In utter amazement, we witnessed a huge display of angel's wings that spanned the sky all the way to the horizon. This wasn't just a little cloud; this was a massive, colorful display that unfolded right before our eyes. The hairs on our necks stood on end as our "Angel Boy" Sean Gabriel gave us a brilliant light show. The clouds slowly turned from a golden glow to a vibrant orange. I took a few photos and posted them on Sean's Facebook page, letting his friends know what had happened.

On that same evening, many of his friends were gathered at a free concert featuring one of Sean's favorite bands, Animal Collective. The Facebook post was seen by several and soon there was a buzz through many in the crowd. Sean was gone. After the concert, a number of these early-twentysomethings pulled together and shared that they "felt" Sean there that night. There was a clear sense to many of them that he was with them at the show. Some described it as magical.

As we transitioned back to our "normal" routine, I dove back into my work as a videographer. It was somewhat comforting to get my head pointed in another direction and focus on something outside of myself. Sleep came with difficulty, and I kept having visions of Sean in the hospital room. We decided to try EMDR therapy, and it truly helped both Cyn and me, especially with sleep issues. For us, the compassionate, highly skilled therapist who administered the sessions was a successful first step into this new world. If you are unfamiliar with EMDR (Eye Movement Desensitization Reprocessing) therapy, I recommend you consider doing a bit of research for providers in your area. It can be very helpful for treating PTSD. It's ideal to look for a therapist who specializes in grief and loss, and who is "certified" as an EMDR practitioner.

One morning about a week after returning home, I woke up pre-dawn and decided to slip into the hot tub for a soak. I walked outside the house and turned the corner to the spa deck when I felt a warm pocket of air around me. It was like I had walked through a heat source. I knew my house; there was nothing at that corner generating heat. It was dark and cool outside, but the warmth was undeniable. I was excited and said simply, "Thank you, Sean." It was another sign.

Do I believe that Sean sends us signs? Absolutely! I've immersed myself in books (it helps my healing) and several authors suggest that it's best to ask for signs and to talk to your child as if they are right there with you (because they are). One night as I was going to bed, I looked at a photo of Sean. I stared so deeply, it felt like I was peering into his sparkling brown eyes. I laid down, turned out the light, and closed my eyes. Within about five minutes those eyes returned to my mental vision. The room was dark, my eyes were closed, but I was "seeing" his eyes and then his face in my mind. It was a vision of Sean, but it wasn't merely a static photograph. I saw his eyes moving and his smile widened. He was right in front of me in 3D form! He was here...or I was *there!*

He then turned for me to follow him. I was "with him" somehow. It was a fully immersive experience. He moved and I moved with him. I don't know how to describe this without it sounding like a science fiction movie, but I was in communication with him without a word being spoken. I knew we were in motion together and I was aware that we were no longer on the physical plane. My heart felt so full of love and excitement in those precious moments. I didn't understand how this could be happening. I truly felt Sean's warmth. There was a playful joy in our movement together. This continued for about ten minutes until I opened my eyes to see where I was. Did I imagine the whole event? What was going on? Upon opening my eyes, the spell was broken. I no longer felt Sean's presence. But I knew that what I had experienced was real. I laid there vibrating with excitement. He was with me...and I was with him, but it wasn't "here"–it was someplace in between. From what I've read, I believe I may have been astral traveling. I haven't been able to recreate it. My deep gaze into Sean's photo somehow opened a door of consciousness that allowed me to step through for a few minutes of bliss. I felt such incredible love in that place.

Grief does strange things to a person. It's made me stretch my mind and allow for signs and bits of communication from Sean. I've done a lot of reading about the afterlife, about signs and synchronicities. I find this comforting as I educate myself about new research in the world of spirit. My wife joined Helping Parents Heal within a couple months of Sean's transition. The organization had scheduled a conference in Phoenix for August 2022 featuring speakers and workshops related to grief, healing, and mediumship. Although I had some doubts, I agreed to attend the conference. It was there that we had a life-changing experience. We made contact with Sean in the most public of ways.

At the conference, psychic medium Fara Gibson held a "group reading" for the parents. Spirit led her over to our side of the ballroom, and during a spontaneous reading, Sean connected. There were more than a dozen surprising and specific points of proof that were infused with Sean's sarcastic sense of humor. Sean told Fara that I had just torn down a deck and replaced it with a new piece of wood that I had screwed up. ("It doesn't even match, Dad!"). That was so amazing, not only because it was so specific and true, but it was said with Sean's way of teasing. He also chided me about my poor guitar playing. ("You couldn't get the barre chords!"). We were so thrilled and comforted by this reading. To be honest, I was a bit of a skeptic when it came to mediumship, but this one reading was so spot on I just had to accept that it was from our boy. In a room of 800 people, all of whom wanted their child to come through...it was Sean who took over in that special moment. Since then, Cyn and I have reached out to other mediums for readings and made connections with Sean and other family members in spirit. While this may be a little "new age" for some, we have found comfort and even humor as we connect to spirit. (We only use mediums who have been vetted through a scientific, double-blind testing process. A list of qualified mediums is available at HelpingParentsHeal.org). The full reading can be viewed on YouTube.

The grieving and healing journey is unique for every person. I heard one of the other dads in our weekly Helping Fathers Heal support group say that we all grieve not just the person, but the unique relationship we had with that person. My wife and I are both dealing with the passing of our only child, yet her grief is different than mine. My grief is unique because she and I had a different set of connections and experiences. Our grief is uniquely our own and it can make us feel completely alone as we sit within it. It's a lonely and solitary experience...but at the same time, it's common to all of us here on Earth. Humanity has been dealing (or not dealing) with the death of loved ones since the beginning of time. But when it's your child...it seems like no one else could possibly understand.

Truth is, no one else DOES understand! People will say things like, "I can't imagine your pain!" That is a true statement, they can't. If you have a friend or family member who comes forth to talk and comfort you, give them credit for their courage. Sometimes they do say things that are comforting. Conversely, people may say things that are not helpful, and they don't understand our reaction. There are times when all I want is to share my feelings and not have someone try to fix it or make sense of it for me.

In our situation, the people we expected to be there for us in solidarity and support, our family, were not there. We got some phone calls from a couple of family members, but the others were completely off the grid. It felt cruel and confusing and only served to compound our feeling of loss. We not only lost our child, but we also lost our sense of family because it was too much for them to deal with. I know I'm not alone. I've heard many grieving dads say the same thing. Friends and family can go dark when you need them the most. Our current culture is woefully deficient when it comes to supporting those in grief. People haven't been taught what to do. So, they often disappear. As a husband, it's painful to watch. I am very aware of my anger and my feelings that my wife's family virtually abandoned her. My reflex is to protect her, but I can't.

To help me heal I have tried to find my "tribe" of courageous and empathetic souls. I have some friends who will stand with me and allow me to feel the way I feel. If there is one thing I know, it's not to give in to the isolation. To any father out there reading this, I recommend that you FIND YOUR PEOPLE and lean on those who have the compassion and strength to be there for you. The loss of our child is a deep pain. Community helps me heal. Love is the answer.

In the end, that's all there is. Pure love.

You don't have to go through this alone.

And you will get through it.

Helping Fathers Heal

4 Peter's Dad, Martin S.

"I loved a boy with the utmost love of which my soul is capable of, and he is taken from me. Yet in the agony of my spirit in surrendering such a treasure, I feel a thousand times richer than if I had never possessed it."
-William Wordsworth

In the early hours of a brutally cold December 18, 2022, my 25-year-old son, Peter Secondo Salvino accidentally fell into the icy waters of Chicago's Diversey Harbor and drowned.

Peter's passing has been a living hell for me, my wife, his sister, and everyone who called Peter a friend. I am writing this exactly one year since Peter passed. These past months have felt like a decade. The agony of this trauma has thrust us into a new reality, and it is not a place we ever wanted to be. Not a single day has passed where I have not been overwhelmed with anguish and tears. I am mortally wounded but I somehow continue, or maybe I am condemned, to walk the Earth. But I must admit that I have learned a few things about grief and loss along the way and I hope that I can help you in some way.

The first lesson I learned is that asking why I suffered this loss is a futile question. At first, I found myself trying to figure out why Peter had to leave us? Like a paperback detective, I desperately tried to make some sense of how the most brilliant person I ever knew suffered such a stupid accident. In the back of my mind, I figured that, if I could solve this riddle, I would win my son back. I quickly realized that my elaborate figuring, what ifs, and maybes resulted in an equation that, in the end, was multiplied by zero. Nothing was going to bring my boy back. No matter the reason I had lost him, I was left with nothing, a void, an eternal zero. But he had lived, and I still loved him. Instead of asking why I started to ask what? What do I have from Peter? What do I do with his memory? How do I continue? How do I honor him?

The greatest job I will ever have is being the father of Peter and his sister Emma. I cannot thank my wife, Mary, enough for this gift. Watching Peter grow from a babe in my arms, to the boy with whom I saw eye to eye, to the 25-year-old man I looked up to in awe was a blessing and a privilege. Although I always felt blessed, I had no idea that we were living in a fleeting golden age.

Our family of four was a tight, happy unit. Peter was a brilliant, kind person who left an impact on everyone he met. He was successful but humble. Genius but never condescending. His smile was contagious. He was tall and handsome. He loved us and we loved him. Now Peter is gone, and we are left with a gaping hole in our hearts and souls.

Upon returning to Chicago from college, and a year working in a laboratory out East, Peter lived for a year with his sister in an apartment in Chicago's Lincoln Park neighborhood. Peter and I saw each other at least weekly, and we were extremely close. He was more than my son; he was my closest male friend and I miss him dearly. He got me and I got him at a level only a father and son can share. To my wife's amazement, I would sometimes say something lost on everyone else, but Peter would understand it without missing a beat. Peter and I were bound by our shared love for adventure and curious natures. He and I spent hours traveling around Chicago looking for new restaurants, attending or watching White Sox and Bears games, or just running errands. All the while we would share a conversation that would drift effortlessly from serious to silly. As it so happened, Peter and I had tickets for a Bears game the day of his passing. At least once a week we would have a long conversation on the telephone in the evening while I drove home from work, and he prepared his dinner. He made contact with his mother or sister almost daily. Peter also remained close with childhood friends and friends from college. He was very resourceful and curious. After his sister married and moved out of their shared apartment, he built numerous pieces of furniture and wired the apartment such that all the lights and appliances could be controlled by voice commands or via the internet. At the time of his death, Peter was a third-year PhD student and candidate studying neuroscience at Northwestern University's Department of Interdepartmental Neuroscience (NUIN). He was also in a long-term relationship with Alex, his girlfriend from college.

In every picture we have of Peter, he is smiling. Those who were truly close to Pete knew that when he smiled in a certain dreamy way a brilliant idea or insight was sure to follow. But if he smiled and laughed slightly to himself, they knew to stand back, for a wonderfully witty sarcastic barb was coming.

I was so proud of Peter and his numerous academic accomplishments. After his passing, I was made even prouder by the number of touching stories shared with us by his peers and friends, of how he willingly helped them with their projects, studies, and personal lives.

I am still too new to this thing called grief to offer any real or deep insight. This trauma is still too fresh and foreign for me to offer much guidance, so I beg patience from you. But I will share what knowledge and insights I have found. The nicest thing said to me was, "If I could bear this pain for you, I would." So, in the spirit of helping you to bear your pain, I will tell you the little that I know about my life of grief so far.

I have a difficult time with the word GRIEF. I find that the term is just too generic for me. This pain is my pain, my loss is my loss. This is my new reality brought on by this terrible trauma. When I hear others talking about grief, my gut reaction is, "How the hell do they know what I am feeling?" This pain is too deep for anyone to know how I feel. Or at least this is how I felt in the beginning. I have learned to cut the world a bit of slack. Grief is indeed too generic to describe my pain, but this is not anybody's fault. We are all limited by the language we speak. Although deep and rich, the English language simply lacks other words to describe this feeling of overwhelming loss. The indigenous Inuit people supposedly have a hundred words to describe snow; yet English lacks other words to describe this sense of loss, helplessness, and complete heartbreak more accurately or in greater detail. Regarding the limitations of our language, it is interesting to note that English lacks a descriptor, such as widow or orphan, for a parent who has lost a child.

Seeking a better term to describe my feelings I came across the Portuguese word *Saudade*, which I think is better than grief as a descriptor of how I feel.

Saudade, Portuguese: (sau-dah-de) An emotional state of melancholic or profoundly nostalgic longing for a beloved yet absent something or someone. It is often associated with a repressed understanding that one might never encounter the recipient of longing ever again. It is a recollection of feelings, experiences, places, or events, often elusive, that cause a sense of separation from the exciting, pleasant, or joyous sensations they once caused. It derives from the Latin word for solitude.

In addition to discovering the word saudade to describe my feelings, I have found expression in poetry and songs. All are attempts to convey feelings and emotions through art. Many songs bring me to tears when I hear them because I have discovered a hidden or deeper meaning about love and loss. The poems that have touched me are too numerous to list. Each speaks to my heart in different ways. Some evoke memories of Peter as a child. Others speak to my loss and/or my longing to change our fate. All uniquely touch and speak to me as only art can, and words can't.

I have not been alone in my grief journey or travels through saudade. My wife, daughter and I have each sought out professional counseling. Each of us has had mixed results. Initially, I sought a grief sherpa to take me through this uncharted land of pain. Eagerly I asked what I needed to do? What steps I should follow? What should I expect? I knew of Kubler-Ross's Seven Stages of Grief: Shock, Denial, Anger, Bargaining, Depression, Reconstruction, and Acceptance, so I figured that a counselor's job was to take me through the stages one by one. I was wrong.

Within a month of Peter's passing, I started meeting with a grief counselor each week via Zoom. Instead of guiding me, my counselor follows me as I try to work out my feelings and insights. I discovered that grief is just too complicated, too chaotic, too messy, too personal, too painful to follow any set path. The so-called stages can come all at once or surprisingly not at all. Some days I just cry for an hour. Other days we joke like old friends. He has not suggested steps I can take but instead, he does point out when my thoughts are incongruous with observations I have already made. He helps but does not judge or tell me what to think.

Working with my counselor has been nice, but it has not helped me to know or judge my progress. Peter's passing changed everything about me and how I relate to the world.

Like many fathers, I am used to leading my family. I am the spider smasher, the provider, the answer man. How can I do my job if I don't know what to expect or where I am?

Fortunately, I came across Helping Fathers Heal (HFH) and their weekly online gathering of fathers. These meetings are where I have found the beginnings of a sense of direction. It is a club none of us would ever join by choice. It is a brotherhood linked by common pain, suffering, and confusion. Each week we gather to hear about each other's discoveries and insights on our individual paths of grief and saudade. Mostly I just listen to what others have to say. I always come away from the meeting with some novel insight or observation.

The most significant observation I got from HFH was from one of the more veteran fathers who shared that he had finally reached a point where he could think of his son and smile instead of cry. I am so very far away from this but smiling instead of crying when I think of Peter has become my goal. It might seem stupid, but this simple insight has made a world of difference. It has allowed me to attempt to accept Peter's passing.

I have learned something else from HFH; I cannot expect to ever heal from losing Peter. Some of the fathers who participate lost their children ten or more years ago and the pain that they feel does not seem to have lessened. Instead of hiding or pretending that everything is alright, they join each week and share their notes from their travels through grief and saudade. This realization is not what anybody wants to hear or learn. I found a quote from Rose Kennedy that says it best. "It has been said that time heals all wounds. I do not agree. The wounds remain. In time, the mind, protecting its sanity, covers them with scar tissue and the pain lessens. But it is never gone."

I liken losing Peter to what I think a traumatic amputation must be like. I am mortally wounded. I feel that I should be dead. But somehow, I am not. Instead, I must learn how to strap on my prosthetic smile and go out into the world each day. I may walk amongst the living, but I will never run among them again.

HFH has also taught me a new way of thinking of Peter's passing. HFH is non-denominational, but we share the belief that our children have not died per se, they transitioned. We discuss the signs we believe our children send us from wherever they are now. Via the parent organization, Helping Parents Heal (HPH), many of us have worked with a medium that has been vetted by the organization. Personally, I have had readings with a few mediums since Peter transitioned. It's not like the movies, but I really think there is something to this medium stuff. Each medium got Peter's name right, but not all of them got everything correct. My wife remains doubtful, but it is interesting to note that three of them said that Peter was "playing cards" with a tall man. My father was tall, and his favorite activity was playing cards with friends and family.

On the topic of signs, I must say that both my wife and I agree that we received at least one clear sign from Peter. We are Catholic and on Ash Wednesday of this year I was feeling particularly low. I have always found solace in the liturgy of Ash Wednesday, "ashes to ashes, dust to dust." I went to church for my ashes and to beg for a sign from Peter. That night around 2:00 or 3:00 a.m. the smoke alarms in our house went off awakening us from a deep sleep. This is something that has never happened in our home. I immediately jumped up and proceeded to inspect our house from top to bottom. No smoke or fire was found, and the alarms stopped after a minute or two. As I went back to bed upset and wondering what had caused the alarms to trip, I remembered my asking Peter for a sign earlier that day. I told my wife that I had asked for a sign from Peter, and I firmly believe that the smoke alarms were a sign from our son, our clever, mischievous, electrical engineer.

The loss of my son has been the most devastating thing to have ever happened to me and my family. My wife lost her son; my daughter, her only sibling; and me, I lost my very best pal. I am too new at this to offer any real advice. But I can speak to what so far has enabled me to get through these sad days. I don't have any expectations that any of my friends actually know what I am going through. Nor, to be honest, do I have any special knowledge about what's going on in their lives. When asked, "How are you doing," I don't pretend that everything is OK. I am grateful that they asked about me and I tell them exactly how I am feeling. Good or bad or wherever in between. I tell them. My good friends are not put off by my honesty. Second, I find solace in art, poetry, and songs. There are no words to describe how I feel so I don't search for them. Instead, I seek that which touches me or reflects my broken soul. I know that I cannot go forward without help. I lean on my wife and daughter and seek the counsel of professionals and other fathers who know firsthand of my trauma. I accept that I will never heal from this loss. Instead, I look to the day when thinking of Peter brings nothing but a smile to my face.

I love and miss him so very much.

*I know
you are gone,
your return
an impossible thing,
and yet I still
search the faces
in a crowd, expecting
to see you smile
as you see me.
-Edward Lee*

5 Ariel's Dad, Ish S.

Auditi Naomi Saleh, the younger of my two daughters, was born on November 05, 2002. Her nickname is Ariel. When she was born, her big sister was an enthusiastic fan of the book, "The Little Mermaid" and insisted that we call her Ariel. Since that day, Ariel has been our pride and joy.

Ariel did not want to stay in her mother's womb full term. She was born 4 weeks early. When I looked at her for the first time, my joy knew no bounds. She is my beautiful bundle of joy, my little princess. My whole life, I have prayed for a daughter like her.

Ariel's early life was challenging. She was born with some issues, and we needed to take her to several doctors for a diagnosis. She was short-statured and needed C supplements. The doctors told us that she would grow up like a normal child at her pace despite her physical issues, and her mental health was excellent.

Ariel had a beautiful mind. She did not talk much but her observation power was amazing. She observed her surroundings well. Many times, Ariel surprised me by mentioning topics to which I thought she was not paying attention. She had an excellent memory. I would often ask her for the details whenever I forgot past events. She always gave me an accurate recollection, regardless of how much time may have passed.

Ariel was a mild-mannered kid, very humble and polite. She filled the space with her presence. Anybody who came close to her was touched by her charming personality and charisma. She was full of humor. Her dry jokes were unparalleled. Her funny comments made me smile for days.

As she started growing up, she became interested in music. On lazy afternoons, I would play music loudly and she would move her body with the rhythm. At night, we used to play soft music so that she could go to sleep. She loved to dance, and her love for dancing started at a young age. She used to watch dance moves on YouTube and show them to me. She also performed at weddings and on celebratory occasions. She did not have any stage fright. I love to watch her dance.

Ariel wanted to be a part of every school event. She signed up for school dramas, school dance events, school debates, Model United Nations, and even her school basketball trials. Her physical difficulties could not stop her from trying. One time, her basketball coach called us and said that Ariel had signed up for the basketball team and the coach could not tell her that he needed taller students for the team. The coach was a great man and made her the team manager. She took her responsibilities as a team manager seriously and helped the coach in any way she could.

Ariel was very persistent. She did not take "no" for an answer. Our subdivision had a swim team for the kids. My older daughter, Ramee, was a swim team member. Ariel wanted to join the team also; however, she didn't know how to swim. I told her that she needed two things before she could join the team. First, she needed to learn how to swim and second, she needed to swim from one end of the swimming pool to the other end. The very next day, Ariel started pushing me to take her to the swimming pool and she was determined to learn how to swim. In just two weeks, she not only learned how to swim but also swam the length of the pool. It was a joy to see her complete the lap. Her face lit up and she was proud of her achievement. She made it on the team!

Ariel had patience. My two daughters desperately wanted a dog, but I was the only one who was saying no. I thought that they would lose interest in a few months and taking care of the dog would be my responsibility. Therefore, my daughters decided that Ariel would be the spokesperson and bring the issue to my attention. Ariel was in the second grade at that time. One fine September evening in 2010, Ariel came to me and explained how much they wanted a dog, while Ramee was standing behind a wall, listening to our conversation. She also told me that they would take care of the dog and agreed to sign a contract with me. I told Ariel that she had just started her school year and she would be busy with school. I said, "Let's discuss this after the end of the school year." For the next nine months, Ariel did not mention the dog. However, the day the school year ended, Ariel came to me and told me that she was ready to discuss having a dog. We got a beautiful rescue dog by Thanksgiving.

Ariel did not want much from this world. She wanted to be treated as a normal kid; she wanted to have friends. The world was cruel to her and did not give her what she asked for because she was different. It used to break my heart seeing her sitting by herself on a bench alone at school. However, Ariel did not accept what the world had to offer her. She created her own world with music and friends online. She created a YouTube channel where she discussed various aspects of teenage life and gave advice. She became a major fan of Korean music (K-POP) and started learning how to speak the Korean language. She took Korean language classes during the pandemic. She even memorized and recited a poem by a Korean poet in Korean for a poetry recital competition and won the grand prize. She made us so proud.

Ariel and I had a special father-daughter bond. I started traveling for work in 2012. I used to stay two weeks out of town and two weeks with her. In 2014, I started accepting assignments in foreign countries. I used to come back home three or four times a year and would stay for two or three weeks. Whenever I was home, we often would go to a nearby Starbucks coffee shop and spend time together. The Starbucks people knew her by her name and always welcomed her with open arms. Once in a while, we used to have the father-daughter shopping spree at the mall and father-daughter dinner at one of her favorite restaurants. If I had known what I know now, I would not accept any foreign assignments. I would have stayed with her to watch her bloom like a flower. I regret that I did not spend enough time with her when she was a teenager. I took everything for granted. I thought my life would remain the same forever, but life had a different plan for me. I will never get back to those golden days to make it right.

I still remember vividly the day we took her to the hospital. The surgery had been planned and coordinated for years. In 2016, Ariel's dentist told us that her upper and lower jaws were not aligned, and a simple surgery could fix the problem. The dentist also suggested that we do the surgery when she turned 18 years old. We scheduled the surgery on June 23, 2021, the day Ariel turned 18 years old... It was a hot Texas day, and everything was as usual. We went to the hospital early in the morning. After three hours, the surgeon came out of the operating room and told us that the surgery went well. We were happy. I had been praying for a complication-free surgery. I thought that my prayer had been answered. Boy, was I wrong! The hospital only allowed one parent with her at night because of the pandemic. So, Ariel's mother, Sabina, decided to stay with her, and I came back home to be with Ramee. I could not sleep that night. I was hoping and praying for a night without any complications, without any phone calls from Sabina. I was wrong again. I woke up early the next morning and was getting ready to go to the hospital when the phone rang. When I saw Sabina's number on my phone, I somehow knew that it was bad news. I answered the phone fearfully. Sabina told me to get back to the hospital quickly and also told me that the doctors were taking her back to the operating room for a second surgery. I knew at that time that I was going to lose her. I knew that I would not bring my baby back to our place. I knew that my prayers would remain unanswered.

As Ariel came back from the operating room, we were told that her left lung had collapsed, and the doctors decided to put her on a ventilator. She was placed in the ICU. The next 23 days were tough for the family. One day, we heard some hopeful news, and the next day all hopes were gone. We slowly watched her slip away and she transitioned on July 16, 2021. She was only eighteen. I learned that day that I was not going to see her for the rest of my life. My baby went back to where she came from.

I was numb for the first month. I was angry. I was fuming with rage, but I did not know who I was angry at. I could not believe it. I did not want to believe that I would not see Ariel anymore. There was excruciating pain in my chest. I was in denial. It felt like nothing was fair in this world. I thought that I was having a nightmare, and I would wake up soon. I wanted to wake up from the nightmare so badly. My memories of her were haunting me. I could not sleep or eat. Simple things seemed so hard to me. I could not stop my tears. I could not provide any emotional support to Sabina or Ramee. I could not look at Ariel's pictures or her videos. I could not go to her room. Her room has remained untouched; the way she left it before going to the hospital. I did not know what to do or where to go. It was very suffocating for me. It felt like somebody put a big boulder on my chest and I could not remove it. There was a vast emptiness in my heart. Nothing mattered to me anymore. I had so much love to give her, but she was not there to take my love. I missed her every day, every hour, every minute, and every second. I wanted my baby back.

At first, I did not look for any support from my family or from my friends. I completely shut myself down. I did not talk much. I did not want to discuss anything about Ariel. I left the room when someone mentioned Ariel. My family and friends visited us for the first two weeks. After that, we were on our own. The three of us just sat down quietly and looked at the wall. Then, someone who had been a family friend for a long time invited us to spend time with them. I did not want to go but Sabina convinced me. We stayed with them for six weeks. Another friend of ours sent several books on mediumship, the afterlife, and grieving, saying that they would be helpful. I didn't even look at those books.

Sabina was very instrumental in finding support for us. She is a strong lady and started to take charge. She found Helping Parents Heal (HPH). She immediately joined. She used to tell me what had been discussed in the meeting and encouraged me to join. She found Helping Fathers Heal (HFH) for me. After three long months, I attended the first meeting on a Wednesday, and it was very enlightening for me. I realized that I was not alone. I started attending the Wednesday calls on a regular basis. However, I did not talk or even turn my camera on for the first few months. I just listened to the other dads. The topics we discussed during the meeting were helpful for me to face my own grief. In 2022 we attended the Helping Parents Heal Conference in Phoenix. I enjoyed meeting other parents and talking to them. I understood their pain and they understood mine. During this long grieving process, I learned that I had lost some old friends, but I gained a lot more new ones.

Sabina started reading books on the afterlife, soul planning, and grieving. She recommended various books to me. I started reading the books one after another, and I found solace in those books. I found hope and I started believing that one day I would meet my daughter again. This hope of meeting her again kept me going. Then, I started to receive signs from Ariel. I have been getting feathers from her when I need her the most, which makes me happy and excited. I know now that she is with me and watching over me. I had never thought about spirituality before Ariel transitioned, but slowly, I gained knowledge. I started to believe that I could communicate with her through a medium or through meditation. The more I read, the more hopeful I became. Now, I am devoted to spirituality. I am certain that life does not end after we transition from this world. Life is eternal.

I had received my fair share of premonitions and strange experiences from the other side of the veil. I did not understand at that time because I had little to no knowledge about the other side. Now, when I look back, I know those were the signs. In 2018, three years before Ariel transitioned, I had a premonition. One afternoon, I was doing my household chores and suddenly, I had a feeling that I was going to lose Ariel when she was 18. It came from deep inside of my heart. I had a feeling that she would not be with us long. I also saw her room without her. Her room would remain empty for a long time. Everything would be there except Ariel. At that time, I did not know anything about souls or master spirit guides. Therefore, I suppressed my feelings. I was ashamed of myself. I was angry with myself. This feeling surfaced in my mind three or four times between 2018 and 2021, but each time I suppressed it. I wasn't paying attention to my inner voice.

I had a shared end-of-life experience the day Ariel transitioned. That afternoon, I was all alone in the hospital room next to Ariel and I dozed off in the chair. I dreamt about a beautiful day. The sun was radiating a bright golden color which I had never seen before. I saw Ariel. She was laughing and joyfully dancing. She was happy. I saw her running fast towards the sun through a beautiful green field. Everything looked so peaceful. I saw incredible colors that I cannot even describe. Then I woke up. Within fifteen minutes, her oxygen level started to drop. She transitioned later that evening.

Sabina also received signs from Ariel and felt her presence. She meditates a lot, and through her meditations, she can communicate with Ariel. She can feel her presence during her evening walk as if Ariel is walking next to her. She can feel Ariel's presence while sleeping as if Ariel is sleeping next to her or giving her a hug.

Ramee gets signs from Ariel through her phone. Her phone starts playing Ariel's favorite songs randomly. She gets unicorn images in her phone. Ariel loves unicorns.

We have had several medium readings, and we were happy with the results. Mediums like Mark Anthony, Kat Baillie, Manisha Akhauri, Isabella Johnson, and several others. Ariel came through during an HFH gallery reading with Christopher Mendez and in an HPH gallery reading with Mark Anthony. They all shared with us things only we knew. It confirms that there is life after transition.

My outlook and perspective about life has changed while I have been going through the grieving process. I firmly believe that we are here for a purpose. We signed contracts to learn specific things before coming to this world and when it is done, we'll go back and meet our loved ones. It may sound surprising, but I am not the same man that I used to be. My outlook, my thoughts, my perspective, and my behavior are totally different now. I believe that our kids are truly master souls. They are incredibly wise and knowledgeable. They came to this world for a specific purpose and went back home after the completion of their tasks. I also believe in a slight modification of the old saying; when one door closes, several other doors open at the same time.

I sincerely do not want anybody to be on the path I am traveling. However, it does not matter what I want or don't want. I believe many of these things are predetermined. My advice to other dads is that the grieving process is one heck of a roller coaster ride. One moment you are laughing and the next moment you are crying. Be brave and be strong. There is light at the end of the long and dark tunnel we are in. It is true that we cannot physically see, touch, or give a hug to our kids but they are always with us. They are letting us know about their presence by giving us signs. And don't forget to ask for help. When you are down or miss your kids badly, ask them to talk to you. They are ready to respond. Life doesn't end after the transition. It continues. Therefore, there is no reason to be disheartened. We will see them again.

6 Nolan's Dad, Warren G.

Nolan was an incredibly gifted and skilled musician, singer, songwriter, arranger, producer, and actor. He had just uploaded his first original song for public release only four weeks before his transition. It went live several weeks after he transitioned. It was hard enough wrestling with the fact that he had passed, let alone that he wasn't here physically to celebrate his song going live to the world. We are so grateful Nolan shared so much of himself through his music. He accomplished this in just 15 years on earth.

Since his passing, my wife and I have continued doing what Nolan intended, to release his original songs and arrangements with help from his coaches, teachers, producers, and friends. He was prolific, having written more than 80 songs and 52 a capella arrangements. Doing this work to release his music has been like a life preserver, helping us keep our heads above water, or like a handrail to hold onto and steady ourselves. And it has kept us in touch with Nolan's people. If you're curious, his music can be found at https://linktr.ee/nolangibbons and anywhere you stream music under his artist name "Nolan Gibbons."

Because he passed during the pandemic, we couldn't have a proper memorial. So, the following summer we decided to hold an outdoor music festival in his honor, which coincided with his 16th birthday. We called it NOLANFEST and held it at our town beach. We rented a stage with lights, hired a proper sound engineer, and invited people from all his communities to come perform and share stories about their time with Nolan. It was so amazing that we made it an annual event as a gift to our community, giving young artists a place to perform and cheer one another on.

We also founded a non-profit called the Nolan Gibbons Memorial Fund (www.nolangibbons.org), to empower young performing artists through grants and scholarships in support of their creative pursuits and passions.

As proud as we are of his musical/artistic accomplishments, we are most proud of the person he is and was in the world. Nolan was kind, empathetic, humble, compassionate, incredibly funny, and always such a cheerleader for the disenfranchised, always helping others feel welcome.

"Nolan was my first friend," is what we've heard from multiple people in every one of his communities. Nolan made sure to welcome the new person and to comfort, reassure, and befriend those who felt they didn't belong. He had a wisdom that didn't match his young age.

Several years prior to Nolan's passing, I was beating myself up for not growing my client base and my business. But my wife woke me up to how fast Nolan's teen years were going to pass us by. Before we knew it, Nolan was going to be all grown up, moved out, and touring in Europe. That was all I needed to hear. I realized how fortunate I was to work for myself and make my own schedule. My new priority was to be there for everything! And I was.

When Nolan became one of the members of AcapopKids (a professional kids a capella group), I got to travel with him all over the country. I was able to be with him at recording studios and music video shoots...even when they appeared on the Kelly Clarkson Show! I was there for all of it. I took him to theater performances and "SHOWSTOPPERS" rehearsals (a community service singing troupe). We saw sooo many musicals! I'm very glad I was a part of it. All that windshield time with Nolan in "Truckie" (his name for my truck) listening to music and talking about how it was put together; it was a gift that I cherish. As father and son, we were very close and did everything together. He was my favorite person.

When he joined AcapopKids, Nolan knew that it would end and that he would age out. We would often remind him, "What do you want to get out of this experience?" And boy did he make the most of it. To watch Nolan work was incredible. He loved all of it: traveling, making music with the other kids, working with choreographers and videographers. Nolan embraced the opportunity and completely immersed himself in audio production. He learned by reverse engineering how the producers would arrange and record songs, and how a music video was shot. He even learned the sheet music software used for sharing arrangements and a capella music. We would stay behind in the recording studio, after Nolan was finished recording his part for a song, just to watch the producers record the other kids and absorb their entire process. Nolan loved everything about making music and worked his butt off doing it.

One day, Nolan and I were in his home studio after yet another moment where he'd blown my mind by sharing his music with me. As we left the studio to take a break and get something to eat, I was so overwhelmed with love for him that I said, "You know I love you, Nolan...and your music is pretty good. But Nolan, I *really* like you." He looked at me with tears welling up and then he grabbed me and hugged me hard. What I'd just said to him, that I really like him, he got it and let it all the way in. I believe he understood what I was saying, that I'm his dad and I'm supposed to love him, but that I LIKE him, too. That was somehow a deeper love. Even though we told each other "I love you" multiple times a day for his entire life, I will forever remember that moment with gratitude.

Nolan passed in his sleep on August 18, 2020, at age 15. With no cause found, and no prior health issues, his passing was classified as Sudden Unexplained Death in Childhood (SUDC https://sudc.org/). We have enrolled in SUDC's research studies to help build their database to hopefully find a cause one day. To me, the reason for his passing was simple: his soul left his body.

The day before Nolan passed was an amazing day. We were all together at home. My wife, Sheila, Nolan, and I were hanging out in the pool talking and laughing. Later, Sheila went out and got us all ice cream. Nolan and I stayed up late watching a funny movie…popcorn, the works.

I even laid down with him when he went to bed, the two of us giggling at TikTok clips. At one point he said, "Hey Daddy! Are you going to sleep here?" I realized I must have been snoring and said "No sweetie. I'll sleep in my bed with Mommy. Good night." It was the only bedtime during his entire life that I didn't say "I love you."

The next day, I was out fishing when I got the call, "This is the town of Marion. You need to get home." When I arrived, the police were at my house. I ran to Nolan's room. And when I saw him, my first words were, "Oh, he's not there." I knew Nolan was gone. It was an immediate and crushing acceptance mixed with disbelief. He was gone, but at the same time, I could still feel him in the room. I immediately began talking to him, saying "It's okay, Nolan. It's okay. Mommy and I are right here." I was trying to comfort him so he wouldn't be scared seeing our terror.

Right away, Sheila and I made grief our full-time job, with everything else taking a back seat. Nothing was more important than grieving…feeling and processing everything was our top priority. We put work on the back burner, doing as little as possible. All we could focus on was processing our grief, trying to understand what had happened, what it meant, and what it didn't.

Whenever our special people would come to our house, we'd tell them that this is how we roll. We talk about Nolan all the time. We cry. We laugh. All of it. All these emotions are present whether we let ourselves feel them consciously or not, so we may as well honor them by feeling them. Otherwise, they will find a way out through the cracks in inconvenient or unhealthy ways.

Everyone copes with grief differently. For us, some people needed to be super busy when they were around us. A special few were amazing at just being with us and doing nothing...nothing! They'd just be with us and whatever we were feeling and talking about. We learned that whenever someone would simply witness our grief, healing would happen.

We've had tremendous support from grief counselors and therapists, and we still meet with them. The online support community, Helping Parents Heal, has been huge for us. My wife encouraged me to join Helping Fathers Heal, which has been the most significant and helpful healing and supportive place for me. I've made many new friends and helped other dads. It's an incredibly loving and safe space for dads going through the unthinkable together.

I have found it is incredibly important to spread your net of support wide. We need way more than just one source of support. Putting all your eggs in one basket is unrealistic and can be a burden on that single source. I continue to collect even more resources for support, even now, three years into my grief journey.

Here are a few resources that have helped me:
- My wife! I'm lucky we can lean on each other, making us closer.
- Helping Parents Heal–it's been a lifesaver.
- Helping Fathers Heal–a game changer for me.
- Therapy–it helps to just talk and let out the feelings. Sort things out.
- Grief counselor–my wife and I see her together, and it doubles as marriage counseling.
- Mediums–we've had some amazing connections with Nolan.
- Family–My older brother has put in the work to learn how to love me and be of support. We have grown closer than ever.
- Passions or hobbies–I began taking saxophone lessons from Nolan's

teacher, Marcus. It's been healing to learn how to do the types of things Nolan loved, and it expands my own connection with him through music.
- Energy work–This includes body work such as The Alexander Technique, as well as, Reiki, which is working with the body's energy. These and other modalities are aimed at healing mind, body, and spirit. Sometimes, I physically feel Nolan's touch during these sessions.
- Male Bonding–This may seem obvious but it's super important. My fishing buddies have been incredibly supportive. Not only do we go fishing, but we have deep, meaningful conversations. It's been hard going back to fishing because that's what I was doing the day I got the call telling me Nolan had passed.

"There's no cheese down that tunnel" is a phrase I use to remind myself that not everyone can be the support I need in the moment and that it's better to accept others as they are.

I've learned that all we really have…really…is just loving each other. Loving each other, helping each other, making a difference for each other… it's our greatest source of fulfillment and it's the only thing we take with us.

Making grieving our full-time priority from the beginning has helped us tremendously. The grief is there whether we accept it or try to ignore it, so we've found it's best to embrace it and be with it.

When I need to talk with someone, I don't wait until my weekly Helping Fathers Heal meeting. I've found it helpful to reach out to my other sources of support whenever I feel it's necessary. I have a new practice; whenever I catch myself thinking of someone, I immediately text them: "I just caught myself thinking of you." By doing this, it helps start conversations that are supportive and healing.

Things that are helpful for a grieving person are beneficial for everyone, even those not grieving:
- recognizing that we need to acknowledge and feel our feelings;

- offering unconditional love and support;
- being there for one another;
- finding your tribe;
- never going it alone;
- recognizing when "there's no cheese down that tunnel";
- accepting others for who they are and who they are not;
- surrendering and accepting what is; and
- witnessing another's grief brings healing.

After a session with Sue Frederick, an Intuitive Coach, Master Numerologist, and Unity Minister (https://careerintuitive.org/about-sue-frederick/), we learned that Nolan had been here before, in a different life, where he already did the "fame" thing. This made sense to us. Over and over, we saw Nolan do things with music that were hard to explain, leaving us wondering out loud, "How is he doing this?" While we never used the word when he was here physically, he was definitely a prodigy.

He always wanted to make the best music possible, or to make a musical theater performance the best possible. He worked so hard, but Nolan had no interest in notoriety or fame.

Many of Nolan's song lyrics are prophetic. I explain it to myself this way: his soul collaborated with his subconscious to write these incredibly prophetic lyrics as a gift to us. They comfort us, showing us his soul knew he would be transitioning. When we first read these lyrics, it was hard to comprehend how a 12- or 13-year-old could write them. One of our favorite songs, "Kaleidoscopes," is all about grief and loss, a gift he left us as if his soul knew what we are going through. There's a video of Nolan performing Kaleidoscopes on an open mic Zoom call where he struggles to explain where the song came from. He said, "I was surprised at what came out."

I didn't realize this until my son passed, but in my adult life I had developed a comfort with being in the midst of things I didn't understand, accepting it, yet not needing to flee or make it wrong. This became incredibly helpful in the ultimate confusion of our son's passing, and the entire grief journey that followed.

Advice for other fathers going through this journey? Don't go it alone. Grief is a team sport. You MUST find your tribe, your people. The dads I meet who are struggling the most are the ones who feel they have to do it alone.

We live in a grief-illiterate culture. Sadly, so many dads suffer from what our culture teaches, that men need to be tough, to be strong, not show emotions, and that vulnerability is somehow a weakness. Our culture associates these human traits with the feminine, and somehow feminine traits are "weak". This misogynist bullshit is just that - bullshit. And it is hurting us.

The reason we have feelings is to FEEL them. That's literally what they are for. Being vulnerable and open to emotions is a superpower, and possibly the bravest thing you can do, and need to do. As Brené Brown says, "There is no courage without vulnerability."

What have been the most helpful practices for my own healing? Early on, my wife and I began doing morning check-ins (something I'd heard about from other dads in Helping Fathers Heal). It's been incredibly helpful and healing. Now, after three years, we check in multiple times a day. We've learned it's a great way to love and support each other, and not just for grief.

Anything that involves talking about Nolan is helpful and healing. Most people's favorite topic is talking about their kids. The same goes for grieving parents, perhaps with a stronger need.

Talking about music and how a song is put together was Nolan's obsession and it was how we bonded the deepest. So, I do this now with others and find it very helpful.

Because Nolan loved to travel, we sent his ashes with his friends and family whenever they traveled somewhere that Nolan wanted to go. So far, his ashes have been spread in Wisconsin, Cape Cod, Iceland, Brazil, The Grand Canyon, Prague (Czech Republic), both campuses of A Capella Academy (the current one at Scripps College and the previous campus at Mount Saint Mary's University - both in L.A.), and in the ink of my wife's tattoo. We've found that this practice of including others to help spread Nolan's ashes is healing for them and us.

Going to the Helping Parents Heal conference in 2022 was incredibly helpful. I'd spent almost two years with these people on Zoom and on the phone, and we were all giddy with excitement and anticipation to meet in person, hug, and talk with each other. I highly recommend it.

Nolan continues to show up in countless ways. We have had numerous signs that blew our minds, showing us that he is with us, and often in incredibly powerful ways. Mediums have been super helpful, especially in the first couple of years as we were finding our feet.

Whenever my wife and I leave the house together in the car, Nolan always shows up. When I feel him, I get super strong "willies"...goosebumps, but from the inside out.

In a dream visitation from Nolan, I was arriving at a concert hall, and as I found my way to my seat, I looked down at the stage and there was Nolan standing by a piano. He was talking with the conductor, along with a huge gospel choir. When I saw him, I began exclaiming to friends in our row "NOLAN! It's NOLAN!" Then, Nolan and I locked eyes as he kept talking to the conductor, shooting me a look as if to say, "Not now Daddy! I'm working!" I would later discover that the entire scene of this dream visitation would become the inspiration for a remix of one of Nolan's songs, "MY TURN (Friends Choir Remix)", along with the accompanying cover art. But it wasn't until AFTER the song was released that I put two and two together and realized that the cover art was what I had seen in my dream visitation.

As we were preparing for the release of this original song, the idea of doing a gospel choir remix came up. The arrangement was created, and we invited people from all of Nolan's communities to record themselves and sing on his song...to be part of the choir. Our intention was to provide healing for Nolan's friends. It was healing for me to see the strong show of support. There were no less than 44 individual voices in that special choir!

Helping Fathers Heal

7 Christian's Dad, Roy S.

Christian Trace Schubert was born on November 2, 1992, in Innisfail, Alberta, Canada. My wife, Sharon, and I already had two sons: our first-born, Travis, and the middle brother, Joel. Christian's brothers adored him, as did relatives and friends. He would light up a room with his smile and never-ending sense of humor. He looked up to his brothers and had a close bond with them.

His character showed up when he was still quite young. Once, at five years old, he was playing with his brothers while we were working in the yard. Christian came to us saying he fell and hurt his arm. The full story was that he fell into a wishing well we had out front. His brother, Joel, had dared him to climb in and he broke his wrist in the process. He masked his pain and didn't complain about it or blame his brother. This was an early example of Christian's toughness, as well as his loyalty and selflessness.

Another thing that endeared Christian to me was that he had quite the sweet tooth (he gets that from me, I guess). He enjoyed candy far more than even his favorite foods. It wasn't particular to Halloween or Christmas; it was year-round. He would hide the candy from his brothers somewhere in his room.

We lived in a small town in Canada, and my company offered me an opportunity to transfer to Australia for four years. Travis said "Okay" right away. Joel did not want to go because "They don't have hockey!" Christian, who was just four at the time, smiled while looking at his brothers and said, "Make it five!" This was in keeping with Christian's playful personality.

He loved sports and was a trash-talk master. Christian talked trash on the court and on the field, but he did it in a humorous way, not maliciously. He could trash talk and smile right at you. And his friends smiled back.

In addition to our shared love of sweets, we shared the same sense of humor: Pink Panther movies; Mr. Bean; Beverley Hills Ninja; Austin Powers; and other films that his mom didn't understand.

Christian was a dog lover, and we had three Shelties during his lifetime: Coco (a female that protected him); Teco (a photogenic alpha dog); and Kai (still a puppy when Christian passed). He was close to all three. In a medium reading in November of 2023, we were told that all three dogs were with him.

In one way, Christian's childhood ended early. In 2002, when he was ten, he and Sharon were in a car crash that hospitalized him for ten days. He had back injuries and intestinal damage. Christian needed significant pain control medications, but he fully recovered. And, as he showed with other setbacks in his life, he did not complain. He was just happy to be home once he was released.

Christian loved snowboarding, and I am an avid skier. We loved going to the mountains in Alberta and British Columbia together. It was just the two of us, and we generated some great memories, including lunch breaks where Christian always ordered french fries with gravy. Now, when I go, I always

7 Christian's Dad, Roy S.

follow that tradition, french fries with gravy. After Christian transitioned, I couldn't go back to the hills for three years. When I finally did, the memories were there; I could feel him teasing me as I rode up on the chairlifts and I felt him racing with me down the slopes. I keep looking for his tracks in the snow.

As he got older, Christian's interests changed. He grew apart from his former best friend and started to run with a different crowd. He was more interested in doing what his new friends were doing.

He showed some signs of mental health issues when he turned 17 years old. He reached out for help, and we tried private counselors. But when he turned 18, we could not force him to do anything. When he received health services after that, he felt what they provided was not beneficial.

In the last few weeks of his life, Christian was very loving and caring with Sharon and the family. On his 20th birthday, none of his "new" friends acknowledged his birthday, but he showed no emotion. Our family went out for his birthday dinner, and then Christian and I went to have a drink at a local establishment.

He mentioned he wanted to make us proud. I replied, "We are already proud of you, son. What can Mom and I do for you to help you achieve your goals?" He said, simply, "I got this, Dad!"

Christian transitioned on January 25, 2013, because of an accidental drug overdose. His alarm clock was repeatedly beeping loudly, and when Joel went in to check on him, he found that Christian had passed beside his bed. His brother was devastated. In the days that followed, Joel was furious with Christian's so-called friends, and with the dealer who had sold him the pill. In a medium reading, Christian told us he was out of his body at the top of the room looking down at his brother.

Those few days are a blur for me. Sharon was at work, and I was in Houston, due to arrive back that evening. Joel called me, then I called Sharon and asked her to get home as quickly as possible. She left work and never went back to that or any other salaried job.

When I got home from Houston, I tried to comfort Sharon. Then I went to Travis and Joel and hugged them both closely. They were both shattered.

Sharon said she would be changed forever. I didn't understand this initially, but I soon learned it changed me forever, as well.

I felt lost, guilty that I could not protect my son. I hadn't been able to save him, and then I felt inadequate in my role as supporter and comforter for my family. The helplessness I felt was debilitating and I was lost in a fog. My energy level plummeted.

Sharon's sister, Marjorie, and brother-in-law, Glenn, flew in that evening from Scottsdale, Arizona to provide support to our family. Glenn helped me with planning the funeral arrangements, which were emotionally hard and exhausting. We both hugged and had a good cry during the arrangements. Looking back, I am so thankful to Glenn and Marjorie for their love and support at that time.

Before Christian's passing, we had planned to go to Mexico for two weeks with his middle brother, Joel, joining us a week into our trip. Christian's older brother, Travis, ended up taking Christian's spot. We all released some ashes into the ocean in memory of Christian, and we all said his name. Sharon said she wanted to go back home. I replied sadly, "Whether in the snow or in the sun, we're grieving."

On the plane ride back, we wore sunglasses, wiped away tears, and looked out the window for signs from Christian.

After our return from Mexico, I traveled back to Houston and dove into my work. I felt enormous guilt that I hadn't been able to protect my son. Sharon was putting a lot of energy into her grieving and healing process, while I was in a fog and grieved in isolation. We worried about Christian's brothers and how we could be there for them emotionally.

After five months, Sharon and I went to grief counseling. We each met with a counselor one-on-one. This did nothing for me; he gave me some pamphlets and said, "This is where you are and the emotions you can expect." It made me angrier. Sharon felt that it helped her, though.

At the same clinic, we went to a parents' support group every week for six weeks. As opposed to the one-on-ones, I found the group sessions much more helpful. However, the group was mostly mothers; there were only

7 Christian's Dad, Roy S.

three other dads. Connecting with the dads was trying at times, as one would dominate and not let others speak. Facilitation of the group was handled by a couple whose son had passed six years earlier. Later in our journey, we reconnected with them and became supportive friends for each other.

Along our grief process, I realized very quickly who was in our support group, and we distanced ourselves from friends and family who were not supportive. Either they did not understand our needs, or they were uncomfortable around us. I was talking to a close relative, and he was surprised that I was still grieving Christian. I told him that the transition of a child is not the same as the passing of a father or mother. I'm doubtful that he "gets it." I have gradually edged that person away from our close circle.

I looked to Sharon to help me understand my grief, but I was not always open to trying what worked for her. I did not really get to mourn my father, who passed just 26 days before Christian. When I was doing something in the garage, I would talk out loud to them both. They were both good with their hands, and I wanted their guidance on how to finish a project. I still do that today; it brings me comfort.

Christian loved Christmas and baking with Sharon for the holidays. The first Christmas after he passed was very difficult with no outdoor lights and no big turkey dinner until Boxing Day. Christian loved to build with Lego blocks, so that Christmas I got a Lego kit of the London Bridge. I worked on it in earnest to get it partially built, but I found it very difficult. I just needed to talk to him, and I believed he would help guide me to complete it.

After he transitioned, Sharon saw signs from Christian immediately. I still carried guilt and was not yet open to signs from him, so I didn't recognize them, even if they were there. Sharon was flying to meet me for a vacation when she believed she saw Christian on the plane, and that young man helped her take things out of the overhead compartment. In a medium reading Sharon had later, Christian said, "If you see me, it's because it is me."

In my grief journey, I did not really have any male support. Only one good friend listened and provided support and camaraderie. I was able to listen to his challenges with his eldest daughter's illness, and he took comfort that I cared and offered support after my own experiences. He appreciated our conversations, and they helped him with his daughter.

Five years on, I finally understood that Christian's passing was not my fault, as I had no control over what happened. So, I let it go. An enormous burden was lifted, and my grief began to heal. I started to recognize the signs. I could be more "present" in enjoying my life. I was able to cry uncontrollably while music played or something on TV triggered me (Sharon calls me "Puddles"). I was able to go to the grocery store and buy his favorite foods and enjoy them and the memories they brought.

Sharon and I have had individual as well as couple's medium readings. From these, we are certain that Christian is fine. At one reading, he even teased me that he was waiting at the bottom of the ski slope while I was slowly coming down. Sharon and I have celebrated Christian's birthday and "angelversary" dates differently each year. As I lost the guilt, it became more about the good memories. Laughter became an increasing part of each celebration.

Sharon and I have had different grief paths. Hers was focused on taking the time for healing. For me, I distracted myself with work, and I was feeling a lot of guilt. With Sharon's help, I later realized that it wasn't my fault. What happened to Christian was out of my control. Although our grief journeys were different, we always wanted to be there for each other and support one another unconditionally.

A few years after Christian's transition, Sharon started going into schools to tell our story with the hope that others could avoid our pain. She received feedback that what she was doing was admirable. Some people came up to thank her for her speech, sharing stories about friends who were on the wrong track. After Sharon's speeches, these people were motivated to intervene and help their friends. She has also volunteered with the same support group we took part in ten years before. I am very proud of Sharon. It takes a lot of energy, courage, and determination to try to make a difference.

It has been ten years now, but not one day goes by without feeling grief and pain about Christian's transition. But I have hope for his signs and I have good memories. I smile knowing that he is looking on, saving my butt as I hurtle down the ski slope!

What have I learned about myself? I now feel good when talking about Christian and sharing his stories. I take comfort in lying on the blankets and pillows Sharon had made from his clothes. Christian loved Hugo Boss designer clothes and wanted to look stylish. I take comfort in knowing the designer clothes I choose to wear are a reminder of the class Christian put on display. I, like Christian, am also a big Philadelphia Eagles fan. It brings me a smile knowing that he is watching the games with me.

In the Helping Fathers Heal group, having more connections with fathers whose children have transitioned, to listen, talk, and share has been a huge blessing for me the last few years. My healing process has taken longer than Sharon's, but we are each still on our paths. The grief will never go away. Having medium sessions lets me know what Christian is doing and where he has traveled, and confirms that he's looking out for his brothers, his sister-in-law, and two nieces. He sends orbs to his oldest brother, Travis, and that brings him comfort and motivation to look for more signs as well.

My advice to new dads on the grief journey is to be patient with yourself and other family members impacted by the loss. You're not going to be the same person that you were before this happened, and that's okay. Over time, you'll move from pure pain to love. The guilt will lift and you will start to notice the signs that your child is still with you. Try to be present. Acknowledge and listen to your heart.

8 Devon's Dad, Jeff H.

Buy the ticket, take the ride...

Devon Hollahan was born on the morning of May 27th, 1987. Fully expecting her first child to be a girl, his mother, Lynn, wasn't sure exactly how to handle the new addition. The first time she changed his diaper, he unleashed a stream of urine onto her chest. Lynn collapsed onto the floor, half laughing and half crying – wondering what exactly she had gotten herself into!

As a child, Devon was quiet, introspective, and occasionally compulsive in his behavior. He would shoot hundreds of basketball shots from the same spot in our driveway. He would incessantly pace or throw balls or other objects against his bedroom wall. At school, he seemed withdrawn at times and didn't have much interaction with his classmates. He was, however, a voracious reader and always had a good book at hand. When he was six or seven, he became interested in dinosaurs and absorbed as much knowledge as he could about them. When watching movies about dinosaurs, he would point out information such as, "The dinosaurs on screen couldn't possibly be there together because the stegosaurus lived during the Jurassic period, while the T-Rex lived during the Cretaceous period." Of course, his career path was already decided; Devon was going to be a paleontologist!

As he grew older, his interests turned to sports. Basketball and baseball became his passions! We followed our local Phoenix Suns and Arizona Diamondbacks and attended as many games as we could. Devon became a statistics nerd, and his mornings usually consisted of him poring over the previous days' box scores and munching on Cheerios with milk dripping off his chin.

When Devon was 12, our family had the chance to go visit his grandparents, Norm and Marian, in New Jersey. One of the highlights of that vacation was a side trip to Boston. Devon and I were invited to join Norm, and many of the executives of Norm's company, to attend a Boston Rex Sox game at famous Fenway Park. During the bus ride to and from the ballpark, Devon entertained the other guests with little-known facts and figures about the Red Sox players. While the other invitees were astounded by the depth and breadth of young Devon's detailed knowledge, his proud father sat back and took it all in!

As he matured, Devon's social skills came along for the ride. He developed some close friends in high school and became more active in extracurricular pursuits. He developed a true love of all things musical. He became proficient on guitar and keyboards. One afternoon, I came home from work to be greeted by the sounds of 'Lady Madonna', by the Beatles. The funny thing was it sounded "live"–note-perfect! The funnier thing was, to the best of my knowledge at the time, I was the only Beatles-loving piano player in the house. Imagine my surprise when I walked into our living room and saw Devon sitting at the piano with his laptop propped on top, playing the complex tune! I asked him, "When did you learn how to play the piano," and "Who in their right mind starts with Lady Madonna?" He casually pointed to his laptop and said, "There's this cool new thing called YouTube and it has piano lessons on it!" I still think of all the money we saved on professional lessons!

It was, however, in college that Devon truly came into his own. He did well enough in his chosen field of study that one of his professors asked Devon to become his teaching assistant. Occasionally, he had the responsibility to conduct classes. Although unsure at first, he took to it quickly and was pretty good at it.

He joined the University of Arizona Ultimate Frisbee Club and, in addition to playing, became the team's unofficial photographer. One afternoon, Devon called home and asked if he could bring a few friends over to the house to sleep over before an Ultimate Frisbee tournament nearby. We were shocked when 20-some-odd Frisbee throwers showed up at our house! Who knew?

The highlight of Devon's collegiate experience was an internship in London the summer before his senior year. Devon had the opportunity to live, work, and bond with 20 of his classmates, and it changed his life. He spoke of his friends often and enthusiastically and had some amazing experiences while abroad. After graduation, when I went down to Tucson to help him with the move back to Scottsdale, we had the opportunity to share a great dinner at a local Mexican restaurant. At that dinner, Devon told me that although he thought his Business Economics degree was valuable, his heart was in teaching. Neither Lynn nor I were surprised because she comes from a long line of educators.

Shortly after Devon's graduation, Lynn and I traveled with friends to the British Virgin Islands for a week-long catamaran trip. Most of that week was spent beyond the range of cell phone signals, so Devon and his sister, Kelsey, were basically left to fend for themselves while we were off playing.

Upon our return, we found out that Devon had applied to, been accepted, and sent payment from his own bank account to the TEFL (Teaching English as a Foreign Language) School in Prague, Czech Republic. His newest adventure was about to begin.

Once again, overseas in Prague, Devon was in his element. There seemed to be an instant bond among the 25 students taking the course together. They studied, dined, partied, and traveled together. Later, one of the course instructors confided to me that there had never been another group that had bonded as closely as this class. During our weekly phone calls with Devon, we heard of his exploits with Domhnall, Jorge, Carrie, Allie, Eliza, Krysten, and others. In early November, our good friends Kelly and Charlotte Smith stopped in Prague to see Devon as part of a broader itinerary and reported that he was as happy, gracious, and animated as they had ever seen him. He was their "tour guide" for the day and showed them some of his favorite spots for dining and sightseeing.

Shortly after that visit, Devon mentioned to us that he was going to Frankfurt, Germany with an acquaintance to see a performance of the American band, "Portugal. The Man." It was to be a quick weekend trip with an overnight stay at a hostel in Frankfurt. We usually called Devon on Sunday mornings, but this particular Sunday, November 22, 2009, he didn't answer his phone. We weren't concerned, because Devon was a seasoned world traveler, and we knew he had been out of town. Later that day, we received the call that would change the course of our lives. Devon's traveling companion called from Prague, saying that he and Devon became separated on their way back to their hostel after the concert. He assumed Devon would show up later, and when he didn't, the acquaintance headed back to Prague, assuming Devon had caught an earlier train. Upon arriving back in Prague and not finding him there either, he assumed Devon was missing and was calling to let us know. Again, we didn't panic at this point because of Devon's extensive travel experience, but it was certainly out of character for him to be out of touch with friends and family for so long.

Over the next week, Devon's disappearance took on a life of its own.

8 Devon's Dad, Jeff H.

With no evidence anywhere about the whereabouts of our son, the local and national media got involved. On Thanksgiving, we had a camera crew from The Today Show in our home. The following day, we did live interviews with all three major television networks. The disappearance of a quiet, somewhat shy, and unassuming young man had become national news.

It was during these early days that Lynn received the call that changed everything. A few days after Devon's disappearance, our home phone rang. Lynn answered the call and the voice on the other end said, "Hello, my name is Debra Martin, and I'm a medium." Debra had found us through a mutual friend, for whom she had recently given a reading. For the next several weeks, Debra became Lynn's "lifeline". Lynn found it very easy to talk with her. She shared her fears and anxieties and found a calm, understanding, and supportive voice on the other end. It was also during one of these early calls that Lynn first heard the phrase "The raven will show you the answer."

As the search for Devon continued, we were contacted by mediums from Russia, Poland, England, Florida, and Tucson, Arizona. Although the messages were different, the common thread through all of them was the same as that from Debra: The raven or blackbird will show you the answer.

Over the next three weeks, we scoured Frankfurt. We had volunteers from the community place fliers at train stations and public places. We formed search parties and walked the neighborhoods at all hours. There were meetings with the police to discuss their findings and we even booked a flight to Prague to go meet Devon's classmates and collect his belongings at his apartment.

As time went by, it became increasingly clear to us that Devon most likely ended up in the Main River in Frankfurt. Upon our return to Germany from Prague, we–as a family–decided there was not much more we could do in Europe and decided to fly home. We did have one more day in Frankfurt and Lynn told us that she had a strong need to go down to the river to say goodbye to our son. On a cold, gray, winter's day in Frankfurt, Lynn, Kelsey and I walked arm-in-arm down to the river. Once there, Kelsey stayed up near street level while Lynn and I walked down to the park area that lined both sides of the river. We were together physically but separated emotionally. Our hopes were dashed. We tried to absorb the events of the last month, the heartbreak, anguish, anger, and confusion. We also reflected on the outpouring of love from friends, family, and total strangers from around the globe who got caught up in our story. The compassion from the staff at the Marriott Hotel—the employees from my firm in Europe, who gave up their precious weekends to help in the search for our son and provide offers of food and lodging.

While we were wandering around the park and pondering our new reality, a large black raven flew down and landed on the grass between us. The raven looked at Lynn and then looked to the river and repeated that motion again and again! Was this the bird the mediums had told us about? Lynn believed it, and even skeptical me was having a hard time discounting it. As if to add an exclamation point to the experience, when Lynn walked down to a spot where she could place her hand in the water, the raven went with her and took a drink each time she touched the surface. With tears in our eyes, we headed back to the hotel and the next morning, we left for home.

Once home, our "odyssey" over, the reality of our new life settled in with a dark heaviness. The first day back, we received a call from the US State Department that a body matching Devon's description was pulled from the Rhine River, 60 kilometers downstream from Frankfurt. Shortly thereafter, dental records confirmed it was Devon. It was December 22nd. Merry Christmas...

On Christmas day, we begrudgingly accepted an invitation to join some extended family for dinner. It was the most awkward family gathering of our lives. Devon's name did not come up, the 800-pound gorilla in the room was ignored. We put our heads down and tried to finish up and leave as quickly as possible.

After the meal, Lynn asked me to read aloud an email that I had received the previous day from Trish, one of Devon's TEFL instructors in Prague. In the letter, she described Devon as a student and person, the gifts and talents he shared, and the special bond that his class had maintained throughout the course. Then, a surprise: Trish mentioned that ever since she was little, when a close relative passed, she would often have a "vision" of that relative and that these visions brought her peace and comfort. She went on to describe a recent vision of Devon. She said the vision took place during the Christmas market in downtown Prague. She mentioned the smell of the pine trees and holiday food from the stalls and that the snow was lightly falling. Across the square, in a crowd of people, she saw Devon and he walked toward her. She described the clothing he was wearing, his backpack, and other traveling essentials and as he drew close, she asked him, "Devon, where have you been? Don't you know everyone is looking for you?" He replied, "Tell them that I am fine and that I've been with them the whole time!"

I was unable to read this straight through due to the continuous flow of tears. When I could focus again, I looked up across the table. Lynn's mother, Marian, had a curious look on her face. She looked over at Norm and asked if he would read a letter he had just received from his granddaughter, Sarah, in San Diego. In this letter, she described a vision she had recently had. In her vision, she was in a Christmas market in a medieval city. She mentioned the cobblestone streets, the smell of food and pine trees, and a crowd of people, from which Devon appeared. As Devon drew near, she described the clothes he was wearing. It was the same outfit he was wearing in Trish's vision. Sarah also asked Devon the same question Trish had and received the same answer: "Tell them I am fine, and I've been with them the whole time." Trish and Sarah didn't know each other. When the dates of the letters were compared, they happened on the same evening, eleven time zones away from each other, and "coincidentally," while Lynn, Kelsey, and I were walking through the Prague Christmas markets. He really HAD been with us the whole time! This really was the first synchronicity that I had experienced, but the proximity to Devon's passing reduced the impact it might otherwise have had. There was more to come.

The first weeks of our journey found Lynn, Kelsey, and I in the same home, but infrequently interacting. I was simply unable to deal with the constant pain I saw in the eyes of my wife and daughter. We were lost as a family, and none of us knew how to cope. The days found us in different rooms of the house with doors closed.

One day, Lynn was sitting at her computer, I was in our music room, and Kelsey was in Devon's bedroom. While working on her computer, Lynn received an email from Debra Martin that said Devon was messing around with Kelsey's computer and causing words to repeat and switching to all caps. Lynn forwarded the email to Kelsey. Within seconds, Kelsey came bounding out of Devon's room confirming the odd behavior of her computer! She had rebooted her laptop a few moments earlier to correct the problems!

My first big sign took place in mid-January. I had two tickets to watch the Phoenix Suns play the Cleveland Cavaliers. It was a game that I had expected to attend with Devon. The Cavaliers were his choice because he had never seen Lebron James play in person. Although I had no interest in attending without my son, Lynn convinced me to go. So, with a friend in tow, we set out for the arena.

When we took our seats, I noticed there was a father and son directly in front of me. The young boy was thrilled to be at the game and the interactions between the two of them were just wonderful. Watching them reminded me so much of the times Devon and I had spent at games when he was young. Late in the contest, the Suns mascot and the team cheerleaders came onto the court to heave t-shirts into the crowd. Devon had often tried to snag one of these shirts but had never been successful. I knew the chances were slim since the cheerleaders didn't really have the ability to hurl a t-shirt 18 rows up, but I silently asked for Devon's help. If I could somehow grab a shirt, I wanted to make sure the young fan in front of me got it. As I finished my silent prayer, the Sun's mascot - a gorilla – walked to center court with an air cannon to launch shirts to the farthest reaches of the arena. At that moment, an amazing calm came over me because I KNEW that the first shirt out of the cannon was coming to me! The gorilla pointed his cannon in all four directions to elicit cheers from each section. I saw it happen before it happened. I moved my head two inches to the left, lifted my right arm as high as I could and seconds after he pulled the trigger, that t-shirt hit my upstretched hand! In one motion, I swept my arm around and handed it to the young boy in front of me. The look on his face was easily worth the price of admission!

Debra Martin filled another very important role for us: she introduced us to Mark and Susie Ireland. Mark is one of the founders of Helping Parents Heal. Shortly after meeting the Irelands, we were introduced to Elizabeth Boisson and the rest of the early members of this esteemed support group of parents who shared the same tragic story. They were all trying to live after the passing of their precious child. This was a true blessing for Lynn and me. We had been to a couple of other grief group meetings and had come away from each not only NOT feeling better, but more lost and confused than before! We had finally found "our people"! In the early days of HPH, we tried to meet every couple of months as a group. These gatherings usually took place at local restaurants and were always boisterous and joyful! The night of our first gathering, I commented to no one in particular that I would be amazed if anyone else in the establishment could guess as to what bond the seven couples at our table shared. Couples whose kids have transitioned from this life are not supposed to be having fun, laughing, sharing memories, and joking with one another, right? Well, this group was celebrating their children; telling stories, sharing memories and the higher vibrations were palpable! And they still are....

As I reflect back on everything that has happened to us (and FOR us) over the past 14 years, I believe the "secret" is that Lynn and I have always supported each other on this journey. We may have had different belief systems at the start and different levels of conviction (or in my case, skepticism) regarding the signs and messages, but we celebrate each time one of us connects with Spirit in some fashion! Lynn has taught me to recognize and embrace the signs that encircle us. We surround ourselves with people who lift us up, who celebrate our weirdness, and who love us unconditionally! Albert Einstein said, "There are only two ways to live your life. One is as though nothing is a miracle. The other is as though everything is a miracle." It's a choice. We have made the choice to believe that our son is still right here with us, and he continues to be a strong communicator to both me and, especially, Lynn. He is our cheerleader, our teacher, and, above all, he's still our son.

We bought the ticket and now we're taking the ride!

9 Kyla's Dad, Jason W.

Hello. My name is Jason. I'm the father of two amazing kids. My daughter, Kyla Elizabeth, is one of the most loving and kind 12-year-olds a parent could ask for. Kyla and her brother have a different biological father. When their mother, Stephanie, and I started dating, Kyla was four years old, and her brother was 16 months. Around four to five months into our relationship, Kyla asked, "Can I call you dad?" At that moment I had the biggest smile and the fullest heart. I looked at her and, of course, replied, "YES!"

From that moment on, Kyla, Stephanie, Konnor (Kyla's brother) and I became a family full of love and support. Kyla–or as we called her Ky, KyKy, or Monkey Girl–was always a shining light with our family, friends, and even perfect strangers! Her smile was contagious, just like her giggle.

Family time was always full of laughter and smiles during game/movie nights. Even when Ky wasn't having the most fun during game nights (like losing to her younger brother at Mario Kart), she could still have a laugh under her breath or say some snide comment that would have the whole family laughing, almost in tears! She would watch movies, and even if they weren't her favorites, she would still join us to enjoy snuggles on the couch under blankets; eating popcorn or some other wonderful treat her mother had made.

We love the outdoors. We love swimming at our local beach, riding dirt bikes, and hiking in the Cascade Mountains. Hiking wasn't Ky's favorite thing to do, but after the first ten minutes of her saying "My legs are tired" and "I'm bored," the scenery would overwhelm her, and she would want us to take pictures of her in the wilderness every other step. We could never say no.

Some of our greatest moments were getting Kyla out of her comfort zone like getting her on a dirt bike for the first time and letting her know that crashing was going to happen. "It's getting back on and doing it again that's important!" I assured her that her dad crashes a few times every time he rides. Falling and getting back up was a small lesson of life!

My favorite memory was seeing her join a basketball team for the first time. At first, she really didn't know what to do. But she advanced so quickly that by the end of the season, she had helped her team win their first tournament with some clutch shots at the free throw line and some great defense!

The morning that I'll never forget is one that I hope will someday fade into a blur. It is the single, most heart-wrenching, traumatic moment in my life. My daily routine after I woke up was to first let the dogs out, and then go to her room to make sure she was awake and getting ready for school. As I approached her room, I heard her alarm radio still going off, which was odd. Upon opening her door, I was shocked to witness what is every parent's worst nightmare. I saw the lifeless little body of what was once such a warm and loving young lady. For my own reasons, I won't go into detail. Suffice it to say that Kyla was found to have passed due to asphyxiation.

I couldn't believe this could happen to such a loving girl. I never imagined that I would have to wake her mother and tell her the news that our baby girl had passed away, and in such a horrible way. That was just over eight

9 Kyla's Dad, Jason W.

months ago now, so I'm pretty new to this journey. The pure emotions of that day are still unfathomable. Since then, it's felt like we are on a rollercoaster ride that we can't escape. It's been really tough.

For the first few weeks, we had family come into town from all over. There were lots of tears, long hugs, and stories of the good times that helped bring some laughter and smiles to a house full of sorrow. Neighborhood friends brought us care packages of food, letters, flowers, and most importantly, the feeling of love and compassion for our broken hearts. Once our family had left, Stephanie and I spent most nights simply trying to sleep. We were getting just three to four hours, at most. We would wake one another up questioning if there was anything we could've done differently. We would think of all the "what ifs."

Now we're a family of three. We wanted to make sure that our son knew how much we love him; that we are always here for him, and that we are here to support him in his journey through this tragedy. How do we move forward with our lives and how can we help our son move forward?

We kept Konnor out of school for almost three weeks. He wanted to return to school, as I did with work. We wanted to see what our new normal would be. Returning to work and school was tough for both of us, but leaving Stephanie at home alone was even harder. I know Stephanie is a strong woman, and she knows I would be home the moment she called for support. Konnor only attended school for a short time before we decided on a homeschool co-op, a small group of families who cooperate in the schooling and management of their kids' educations in true "it takes a village" fashion. The students at Konnor's public school had been cruel about the way his sister had passed. This homeschool choice was better for him emotionally, and a more hands-on learning experience for him in a supportive environment.

We received support from our neighbors, family, and school board members. I'm proud to say that after this life-changing experience, Stephanie became a member of the school board "Mental Health Committee" and has been attending all the meetings, even over the summer. Stephanie and Konnor are both talking with counselors. I haven't found counseling yet, but I'm working on not sweating the small things, and just letting life move forward. I'm striving to help my family move forward. I wish this wouldn't have happened to us, or to any parents. This pain isn't something I would wish upon anyone.

While looking for counseling, Stephanie and I found Helping Parents Heal and then, Helping Fathers Heal. Since my first meeting with HFH, I have yet to miss a meeting, and it's hugely therapeutic expressing the good and the bad since Kyla's transition. Our friends and family continue to be hugely supportive. But we've had to distance ourselves from some friends just because of the drama they have in their own lives. It wasn't an easy choice to make, but it is what was needed for healing.

I've learned much on this journey:
- I understand that we will only move forward together if we stay close as a family, not just individually.
- Questions should be asked out loud, not kept inside.
- I am more open to expressing my emotions.
- I'm a better, more patient listener.
- My family is everything, and even though we are spread across the country, we all know we have each other during the good and bad times.

Twelve days after our daughter's passing, my family also lost our father from dementia and throat cancer at 74 years old. This was a blow to me and my three brothers. I still apologize to "Pops" for not being able to fully grieve his passing because I'm still grieving for Kyla. I know they're together and waiting for our time to be reunited in Spirit.

Some of our family and friends have built tributes to Kyla in their homes and on their properties. These have been very touching and healing for us. For example, the mother of one of Kyla's girlfriends was building a chicken coop. A chick was born the same day Kyla passed. They named the chick Kyla, even before they had heard the news of her passing, a wonderful synchronicity. Once they heard about it, they decided to paint the chicken coop hot pink (Ky's favorite color).

We've just passed Ky's 13th birthday. Our close family was here to

9 Kyla's Dad, Jason W.

celebrate. It was a hard "first" without Ky. We did all we could to smile and laugh, to bring joy, and to be thankful. We asked one of Ky's friends to join us at the State Fair. She talked Konnor into going on almost every scary ride he'd never been on. (I am sure it was a shove from his sister above). Just knowing how far Ky's reach goes, with the unconditional love she had for her family and friends, still touches my heart every day.

Words of advice for parents going through the loss of a child:

- Talk, cry, and let your emotions out. Keeping them in will just cause them to build up, and when they do come out, it will be when you least expect it. Talking about my emotions is stress relief, and I feel a weight lifted off my shoulders.

- Sharing your heart with a complete stranger can be healing and can create a new friendship.

- Keep your head up. Stay as positive as possible. Find the silver lining by remembering your child's love and light. Be gentle with yourself on the hard days.

- Find a ritual or a habit. I still go into Ky's bedroom every morning after letting the dogs out. I open her curtains, tell her "Good Day" and that I love and miss her. Every day when I get home from work, I go to her room and say, "Hello, I hope you had a good day." I kiss her picture, then I shut her door. At night I return to her room to wish her sweet dreams and a good night. I say, "I love you always and forever," then I close her curtains, give her picture another goodnight kiss, and shut her door.

- Memorialize your child. I have Kyla's name tattooed on my left wrist. The tattoo is in her handwriting and was done by her loving mother. I'm sure once Konnor is of age, he'll be getting one as well. Eventually, we plan to make her room a place of remembrance, including tie-dye and pink paint. We'll paint ivy on the walls because Kyla was all about the aesthetic in her room. She absolutely loved that word "aesthetic". I believe she truly was an old soul and a hippie at heart!

My first experience with a sign was two weeks after Ky's celebration of life. We had put all the pink heart balloons in her room because they were her favorite color. All the balloons were in one corner of the ceiling of her bedroom. One day I went in to do my usual "good day, love you" routine, and as I was walking out, one balloon came down out of the bunch. It floated down right in front of me. It was the only balloon that had any writing on it; it said, "I LOVE YOU". The balloon stayed at eye level and was there until I closed the door!

I went to the bedroom and grabbed Stephanie to tell her about it. We went back to Kyla's room. The balloon was still at eye level, just where I'd left it. As Stephanie walked into the room, the balloon turned and floated gently to the opposite corner from all the other balloons. It floated side to side above the vanity where Kyla used to do her make-up. It kept dancing side to side, as if under some magical control. It finally stopped a few inches above the vanity and is still there to this day. Stephanie and I looked at each other with tears in our eyes and said "Love you too! Talk to you later." We gave each other huge hugs and just embraced the moment!

I have yet to have any visions or dreams about Ky. I rarely recall dreams, and if I do, they come as déjà vu during the day. Stephanie and I are going to try a medium in the next couple of months as a birthday gift to each other.

Four months after Ky's passing, I was out in the backyard doing some gardening. I kept finding randomly shaped bricks and rocks. Then an idea hit me: Why don't I make a rock garden in tribute to Kyla? I started right then. I used the bricks to create a heart shape. Then, I filled in the space inside the bricks with red lava rocks. It surprised me how much the physical work and the mission soothed me.

When they got wind of my project, Stephanie's dad and stepmom brought over a metal bench with dragonflies in the armrests, plus some ferns and wild grasses. The ferns and grasses are growing now. I spend a lot of time in Kyla's room. From her window, I can look out over the garden.

So, was the idea that "hit me" my own idea? Or someone else's?
KYLA, LOVE YOU ALWAYS AND FOREVER,
YOUR DAD!!!

10 Ryan's Dad, Mike D.

Brandon

Mike with Ryan

This is Ryan's story.

I met Ryan in 1999 when I started to date his mom, Annette. At first, I was not welcomed. But a few years into our relationship, Ryan and I became closer.

When we met, he was 12 years old and loved playing football, baseball, and basketball. He always wanted to be the big man on campus. Always first! He got upset with himself when a game wasn't going well.

When Ryan was 15, he and I decided to restore a classic Chevrolet Chevelle so he could use it to drive to high school. We spent many nights in the garage, cleaning and painting his car, and building the engine. By the time he turned 16, we had built a beautiful car. He was so proud of it.

One day, he came to me and said, "I want to put bucket seats in my car." I answered, "Think about this: you and your girlfriend driving around with all your buddies. When you pick up your girlfriend, where is she going to sit? Will she sit between a couple of your buddies in the back seat? Or are you going to make 'Your Boys' sit together in the back seat? If you leave the bench seat, your girl can be right next to you." A couple of days went by and Ryan said to me, "You're right. I'll keep the seat as it is."

Ryan had a huge heart and a sincere "give-you-the-shirt-off-his-back" attitude. He came home from high school one day, ran to Annette, and declared, "We need to go get Brandon." Brandon was Ryan's best friend. He continued, "He is sleeping in the park-and-ride in his car and showering in the locker room before school."

Annette asked, "Why is he doing that?"

Ryan replied, "His mom had a stroke a week ago and they lost everything."

We agreed to take Brandon in and allowed him to stay with us while his mother recovered, but it turned out to be almost two years before she was able to get back on her feet again. Brandon was just like one of our kids, and he and Ryan became more like brothers than friends.

Ryan was a three-sport athlete, so we traveled to many games and tournaments. Just before he went off to college, we found out he had Factor V, a blood clotting disorder. We discovered he had a blood clot in the vein of his right arm, which required surgery. Further examinations revealed another five pulmonary embolisms. That meant the full-ride scholarship to Utah for football was out of the question. Ryan was devastated by the loss of his football dreams, as well as the scholarship. But he compensated for it by shifting his academic focus to the business side of football. He did end up playing baseball for a couple of years at Northwood University in Michigan, where he earned a dual bachelor's degree in business and marketing. In the meantime, Annette and I had decided to make the move from our home in Michigan to seek better career opportunities in Arizona.

10 Ryan's Dad, Mike D.

When we went back to Michigan for Ryan's college graduation, he pleaded with Annette, "Please don't go back to Arizona! I miss you guys." Annette replied, "Instead of us moving back here to Michigan, why don't you move to Arizona where you will have so many more opportunities?"

A few weeks later, we got a call from Ryan. He and a friend were on their way to Arizona, stopping along the way to see famous baseball parks and watch some great players.

Ryan arrived in Peoria (that's Peoria, Arizona, not Illinois!) and unpacked his belongings. I came home from work the next day and told Ryan, "Pack an overnight bag, we're going to Vegas!" As we drove and approached the outskirts of Las Vegas just after dusk, Ryan looked out the window and asked, "What is that?" There was what looked like a blanket of light glowing in the sky as we came over the mountains.

"That's Vegas!" I replied.

We had a blast that weekend. We were in the Flamingo casino when Ryan turned to me and said, "Mike, I have loved you from the first time I met you." We hugged and continued to play beer pong at O'Shea's. I remember this trip like it was yesterday.

On the 6th of March 2020, I was at the local college signing up for classes to support a career change I had planned after our move to Arizona. I was waiting for my meeting with the counselor when a call came in from my wife's phone. A man's voice came on and told me he was a Chandler police officer. He then said I needed to come home right away.

I ran out, jumped in my truck, and made it home in minutes. There, I found my Annette on the floor, crying her eyes out. The officer pulled me aside and explained that Ryan had passed away that morning. His three-year-old daughter had been with him earlier, but she was safe at home with her mother by this point. Later, we found out that Ryan had purchased what he thought was Xanax during a recent trip to Mexico. However, it wasn't Xanax. It was fentanyl. And it was a fatal dose.

The days following his transition were very hard. At one point, we had to turn off our phones. It was overwhelming to recall the events for each person that Ryan had touched. For seven days we hardly ate or slept.

Family and friends flew in to help with arrangements, so in the first few days we emptied out his home and put his belongings into safe storage. I don't believe Annette and I could have done it alone. The realization of waking up each day without our son was devastating for both of us.

At first, I was the strong one, the one who had to keep everything moving. Annette, on the other hand, felt like she was just ready to die. We had to sell everything our son had worked so hard for in order to provide for his three-year-old daughter and her mother.

The first year or so was just a blur. I ended up going back to work after a couple of months. We were in lockdown because of COVID, and I was drinking myself to death, all the while knowing I had to be there for Annette.

On Ryan's second "Angelversary", Brandon came to visit us in Arizona. We talked Brandon into moving to Arizona to start a new life. Just eight months earlier he had lost his biological mother to COVID, and he was not dealing well with the loss. He was drinking every day and losing weight fast. By that time, he had lost about 70 pounds. He went back to Texas to pack up and sub-lease his apartment. But just twelve days after he left us, we found out he had had a heart attack. He was only 36 years old. We believe this was caused by both the loss of his "brother" Ryan and his biological mother. Or, quite literally, he died of a broken heart.

I had suffered major losses in my life prior to Ryan's passing. I lost my dad in an accident when I was 18, and I had to claim his body. I lost my girlfriend and unborn daughter in a car accident when I was 20. So, I knew what grief was. I just didn't realize the effects it could have on friends and family. The aftermath of losing a child that you've helped to raise for 20+ years really messes you up. I believe I am still angry at all the "what ifs" and the "we never got to see him do _____." The thing that surprised me the most was how people that you thought you were close to became distant, and we didn't know why. We understood later that it was because they didn't know what to say.

One day, a friend of Ryan's talked Annette into having a group phone call

10 Ryan's Dad, Mike D.

with Fara Gibson, a local psychic medium. Annette participated in the call, and later I listened back to the recording with tears in my eyes and disbelief at the accuracy concerning Ryan. Fara told my wife about the upcoming Helping Parents Heal conference to be held in Phoenix. It was sold out, but Fara told us to get on the waiting list, and that she would be there.

Three weeks before the conference, an email popped up on my wife's phone saying that ten tickets had freed up. She quickly jumped online and bought two! The conference was amazing. I met so many people who understood what I was going through. We could talk freely and without a second of fear about making them uncomfortable. One evening, a medium "scramble" was scheduled to be held in four different rooms with two mediums in each. On the way to the session, Annette said out loud, "Ryan, for the first time in my life, I want to be first. You and Brandon need to be loud, be first!" She knew they always wanted to be first in everything they did, so why not here, right now?

We made it to the session just in time to grab our seats. The two mediums came out and introduced themselves. Fara Gibson was one of them. She kicked off her flip-flops, and immediately said, "I'm sorry to just jump in so fast, but I have someone that is being very loud and wants to be first." Then she pointed to Annette and said, "You have two boys in heaven." As she said this, she was coming down off the stage toward us. She reached out her hand to Annette and said, "I have lots to talk about with you, but I'm being pulled in another direction." Annette said, "No worries, you gave me the sign I asked for, and we have another reading with you in October." Fara jokingly replied, "Shut the f**k up!" and walked off to continue with other readings.

As for other signs, the bedroom TV came on by itself the first night Annette was able to go to bed after Ryan's passing. Our china cabinet lights go on without touching them. And my craps table LED lights keep turning on by themselves.

One day, Annette was on the treadmill and got a message from Ryan. She called it a "download" of information. She was getting thoughts of all the good things that had happened since Ryan passed; all the relationships that were repaired and bad feelings set aside to support each other. She cried out loud, "I would give it all back if we could have you back!" Just as she said the words, she lost her balance and stumbled off the treadmill. Why? She had heard Ryan reply, "MOM, stop being so selfish, don't you understand it's all about LOVE?" Those were not her words. She doesn't talk like that.

After the conference, I joined the Helping Fathers Heal Group, where I met some great new brothers. We hold a Zoom meeting every week where we get to talk and tell our stories with nothing but love. This group is what has helped me the most with all my struggles. The men in this group understand that we need to be vulnerable and break down sometimes. We talk about our kids and the difficult life events we're going through.

I had a recent meeting with some of the HFH dads at our car dealership near Phoenix. Fara agreed to join us and gave readings to all nine dads who showed up. She has an incredible accuracy record. It was an amazing experience for each of the dads who attended.

For anyone suffering the loss of a child, my only advice is to find a group that can relate to your situation, and then get involved. One way I found some peace after two years of grieving the passing of Ryan and Brandon was to start a blog. It's designed to raise awareness about fentanyl and the devastating impact it's had on our country. You can read more at www.drsills12.org. If fentanyl has touched your life in some way, share your story. It helps to share what's on your heart and mind. As David Kessler wrote in his book "Finding Meaning", our grief needs to be witnessed.

When our kids pass before us it upsets the natural order of things, but I now know that it was all planned out beforehand, and we agreed to learn this lesson. We come into this life with a "soul plan," and our time to leave this life is always in perfect harmony with that contract. At least, that's what I believe. We somehow agreed to learn this lesson.

11 Autumn's Dad, Mike J.

You do not know me, and I do not know you, but it's likely we share this: we have both experienced the worst thing that can happen to a parent. To have experienced the passing of your own child, a part of you that will never be replaced.

Right now, you are thinking to yourself, "Can anyone fathom the depths I am in right now?" I can. I have been there. I am still there. I will not lie to you and say it gets better. I will tell you it changes. I will hopefully provide you with some information that will help you as you deal with this tragic event: one story; one bit of advice; or one technique that may soften the blow you have experienced. If I can do that, then I have achieved my goal.

My name is Mike, and I am the proud father of the one they called "The Good Samaritan." Her name is Autumn Marie Johnson. She lived her life,

"FULL YEET!" (a.k.a. Full Tilt). She is a savior to animals and a joy to know. Here is my story and what I have learned to date.

As parents know, kids at 16 often go their own way. You are no longer cool or needed as a parent. This was not the case with Autumn. Our relationship never had speed bumps. The year she left for college (2019), she would come out to the garden while I was working, and she would ask if she could do anything to help. I always said no, to which she responded, "Then I am going to sit here with you until you give me something to do." And she sat with me, just to be next to me, just to keep me company.

I often remark, "I won the child lottery!" We have been blessed with three great children. And Autumn, I always knew she was not an ordinary child.

Autumn has always been at the top of her class, taking high school classes in middle school, taking college courses in high school, and graduating summa cum laude. She took 24 college credits during one semester in high school and graduated with the most credits in her school's history. She went for three years to middle school where she didn't get one answer wrong on any quiz or test. Three years, none wrong.

In 2019, Autumn was accepted to Kansas State University. Her dream was to build the best veterinary clinic designed to look like a big red barn. During the summers before college, she worked at a trauma vet clinic in Wasilla, Alaska. Most people cannot handle the pace and caseload of this clinic. Autumn thrived on it. Many nights she would not come home after her shift, and we would stay up worrying about her. She would come through the door past midnight with stories of saving dogs. She would clock out at the end of her shift, and then go back into the surgery to help the doctors. One time she stayed so long, and missed so many meals during the day, that midway through a multi-hour surgery, she went into the bathroom and passed out. The girl has no quit in her. She is all heart and soul.

She never saw an ugly dog. She would say, "Dad, that dog is so cute." I would reply, "No Autumn, that dog is ugly!" "No Dad, all dogs are cute!" Now I get it. Now I understand what she meant. She never looked at the dog's

11 Autumn's Dad, Mike J.

appearance. She only saw their soul. Just as she did with people. She saw your heart and soul. Everyone was beautiful to her. And I know this to be true; if the man who killed her was in need, she would help him out. That's who Autumn is. She is quick to help anyone out. And in the end, that took her life.

By 2021, Autumn was well into her college life. After Thanksgiving, Autumn dropped her boyfriend off at the Kansas City airport. She had just spoken to my wife, Darlene. She said she was on her way "home" from the airport. That is important because "home" was always Alaska. Any other time she spoke of her residence it was always "dorm" or "apartment." This time she said "HOME." This will mean more to the reader later in the story.

Autumn fueled up in Topeka and got back on I-70. A vehicle rollover at the side of the road in the opposite lane just west of Topeka made her stop. She pulled over and waited by her Jeep to cross the road. As the right lane traffic stopped to let her pass, she ran across the highway. As she reached the other lane, she was struck by a twenty-six-foot truck going at full speed. From all accounts, no one saw the truck coming, and all said it was going too fast through a developed accident scene.

Darlene and our youngest son were out shopping and called Autumn, knowing that she was on her way home from the airport. A social worker at the hospital answered Autumn's cell phone. Immediately, my son called me and said something was wrong. But the voice didn't sound like my son's voice. I almost hung up because I thought he was joking. He was feeding me information as Darlene was getting it from the hospital. My only daughter had been in an accident, hit by a semi-truck, and was in surgery. My son was relaying this to me hysterically.

I dropped to the ground, tears rolling down my face. I knew the ending. I was told the ending a long time ago. You see, years before I was "given" a feeling of what would happen, and how. I somehow "knew" that Autumn would pass while driving her Jeep on I-70 near the KC Airport.

Every part of me turned dark and empty. I wanted to kill the driver. I wanted to kill her boyfriend for putting her on the road. I wanted to kill myself. My mind could not grasp what I was hearing. Many thoughts ran through my head; how could someone so vibrant pass away? She had just turned 21. She would be on her way home to Alaska in a few days. Why was she on that road? What about all the dreams I had for her?

She was a huge part of my life plans. I was never going to get back what was lost. I will never make another memory with her. My only girl, I would never hear her voice again. She would never write me another Father's Day card. Autumn is my best friend and biggest cheerleader. How would I survive this?

Darlene returned and called the hospital. I was on the ground, crying, slamming my fists to the floor yelling "FUCK" over and over until my voice gave out. I didn't know what else to do. I felt a sickness I knew I would never get over. I had a knowing that this feeling of staggering loss would be with me until the day I died.

Darlene, on the phone with the surgeon, remained remarkably calm. I heard her ask some questions of the surgeon and knew what had happened. In the end, they could not stop the bleeding and Autumn passed (went "HOME") at 1800 Central Standard Time, surrounded by a team of 17 doctors. In that moment, I passed with her. I didn't follow her, but I felt as if I had. I could only think of my girl being alone, taking the journey by herself. I made one call–the hardest of my life. I had to tell my oldest son, who was stationed in Texas and en route to be with family. I called and let him know his sister had passed, and that he could turn around and return to the base.

She was thereafter known as "The Good Samaritan." Her story made national news. Two days later, as the doctors recalled the situation, they were brought to tears. They told us they tried hard because she was a "go-to" person. I asked what that meant. They said a lot of people run away from those situations because they don't know what to do or are scared. A certain breed of people GO TO the chaos. Autumn moved to the sound of chaos with the goal of helping...people and animals.

She was studying to be an orthopedic veterinary surgeon. She was going to change the vet world. Her effort and skill were admired and copied by those around her.

11 Autumn's Dad, Mike J.

On December 6th, I contacted five friends whose children had also passed. I asked them one simple question, "How did you survive?" They were all consistent with the answer, "Mike, I don't know." Hopefully, I will do better than that for you. As I sit down and write this, my eyes moistening the keyboard, I wish for you to get something, however small, that will help you in your journey.

I take the blame for her passing on many levels. First, I taught her to never leave someone in need. I sent her to every first aid/wilderness survival/Emergency Medical Technician course I could. I blamed myself because I knew where and how it was going to happen and I could not stop it. I blamed myself for not getting her a new Jeep that would have been faster, and she would have been ahead of the traffic accident. I blame myself for not pushing her to go to UC Davis for her schooling. I blamed myself for not telling her to get rid of her boyfriend. I blamed myself for letting her boyfriend put her on the road to the airport. So many things. Of course, none of that is logical. But early in the process, you take the blame for everything.

You find – I found – that nothing else matters. What you worried about yesterday means nothing. Something broken in the house, your job, your appearance, your plans? It's all gone or doesn't matter anymore. You become anti-social because you just don't want to tell the story again. Two years later and I still cry when I talk about Autumn. And when the day comes that I do not cry, I will cry.

Only Darlene was closer to Autumn than I was. And that puts me in a difficult position. How could I comfort Darlene and the boys when I was so utterly devastated? I could not. So, I withdrew and began working tirelessly on her case. I could not comfort my family; I didn't know how.

There are no words that describe a parent whose child is deceased. The English language simply does not have a word or sentence to capture what it is like.

Be kind to yourself, taking blame for it will not change a thing.

Most people who know me say, "I can only imagine the pain you are going through." Respectfully, no. No, you cannot. You see, I "imagined" what it would be like to lose a child. And the reality is far deeper and darker than I had ever imagined. The depth and breadth of the pain defies explanation. And that is what I struggle with so often. People imply that I should be "good" after a year; that I should "just get over it." No, none of that will ever happen. I will never be good with what happened and how it went down. I will never get over my girl getting robbed of her future. Every day, I must fight to stay "in the light." Every day, I must find a reason to continue. Every day, I struggle with what happened. The dark thoughts come. Some days, they are dark even by my standards.

This, at age 54, is the first true loss I have had. All others were expected. I deployed to combat four times and was a state trooper for five years. I have seen my share of losses. I have always thought of Autumn as the one that would get me through the tough times.

I learned that you must find something positive to do each day. Help one person out, or one animal, or do one thing for the planet, however small. It will help.

I began researching the accident within hours. Something was not right. It was at that point I promised my girl that–whatever the cost–I would get her justice. Since that day, I have been the lead investigator for the accident, providing the troopers with video, testimony, and accident site reconstruction. For the first 16 months, it was a 40-hour-a-week effort. A grieving father should not have to do the investigation of his daughter's accident. I should not have to know how many G-forces impacted her. I shouldn't have to listen to all the 911 calls.

Make it known that you are going to advocate for your child. No one else will advocate as well as you can. As I have told the troopers, "I will not quit, give up or fail my daughter." They didn't believe me in the beginning. At this writing, my pursuit of justice continues. The outcome is pending a trial.

When this is done, I will start a foundation in Autumn's name. Autumn's boss at Tier One Veterinary Clinic often said, "If I had ten Autumns I would take over the world." Autumn received no scholarships on her way to college, but I want to provide ten full-ride scholarships to students to ensure that

11 Autumn's Dad, Mike J.

Autumn's legacy continues.

Although she lives on in my memory always, to date I have not dreamed of her. I did have a single visitation on the 420th day. On that day, Autumn showed up as a six-year-old. She needed help putting a folding chair on a high shelf. I lifted her up by her legs so she could put it away. As I brought her back down, I sat on the floor with her in my arms. I turned to Darlene, who was in the room, and I asked, "How is this possible?" But when I looked back at Autumn, she faded and disappeared.

Before she passed, while I was at the trooper academy in Sitka, Autumn sent me a postcard that said, "If I could be anything I would be an eagle so I could fly to you." After she passed, I began seeing eagles when I thought about her. I wanted to see if this was really Autumn's work, so I asked her to show me two eagles at the same time over the Parks Highway. Within a few minutes, as I approached the highway, two eagles were circling above. Three weeks later, a medium told me that the eagles were a sign from her, so I decided to throw down the gauntlet. I got in my truck and headed towards the Parks Highway. I told her, "Autumn–if it is you, send me three eagles over the highway." I know this is impossible. Eagles do not travel together; to see two is rare and three is impossible. I have been in Alaska for 21 years and have never seen three eagles together in the valley. I drove to the Parks, got a phone call, and pulled over. While on the phone I did something I haven't done since posting about Autumn's death: I opened up Facebook. There, I saw a friend's posting of two eagles in his backyard. I was like, "Dang, Autumn. Close!" I scrolled down the page and the first response was a picture of another eagle. Three eagles...in the Park...on my phone. She did it! She did the impossible.

Know that nothing is impossible for your child. Look for signs coming in unexpected ways. I expected her to show me three eagles flying over the Parks. I got three eagles in a different way, but in a way that she knew I would not miss them.

Two years before Autumn left this world, I wrote her a book that included "365 Days of Enlightenment" where I would give her one uplifting saying, a motivational story, or a cool video to watch, each day for a year.

When the year concluded she sent me something to think about. It says:

"Every day is a blessing & should be treated as such. With every sunrise comes the beginning of a new day. Make that New Day Yours!

1. *See something that amazes you.*
2. *Hear something that makes you question reality.*
3. *Feel something that isn't tangible.*
4. *Speak something that inspires those around you.*
5. *Do something that scares you.*
6. *Make something you are proud of.*
7. *Read something that gives you hope.*
8. *Remember something that makes you smile.*
9. *Protect something or someone that you love.*
10. *Be someone that is irreplaceable.*

Because when you live everyday like its your last, your mind is set free of worries."

- Autumn Johnson

This gives me hope. I encourage you to find hope wherever you can.

A few additional bits of advice from a grieving father:
- People will treat you differently. Don't judge them for it.
- Allow others to help you. If not for your sake, for theirs. For some, it may be the only way they know how to help you.
- Few people will know the right thing to say.
- People will say the wrong thing. Don't hold it against them.
- We all grieve differently. Grieve in your own way but do no harm.
- Don't be too proud to ask for help. It doesn't make you weak. It makes you human.
- Never forget, you are not alone.

11 Autumn's Dad, Mike J.

When mourning the passing of someone close, realize this: they are not suffering now, only you are. Death is only seen from your eyes. They were not present on death's arrival. As Epicurus said, "Death does not concern us, because as long as we exist, death is not here. And when it does come, we no longer exist." Instead of using their passing to mourn your loss, use it to celebrate their life. Enjoy what great memories you have of them and everything you have learned from them.

I must look back and say that God blessed us with Autumn for 21 years. I made the most of those years, as she did. She lived a lifetime in those years. She loved a lifetime in those years. She is loved forever.

I pen these words with tears in my eyes, a heavy heart, and a hope that you will get something out of this that may make the journey just a little easier. May God comfort you in this most difficult of times.

12 Zach's Dad, Jerry C.

Zach and I were best friends. This may not have been true during his teen years, (even though he was a great teenager and didn't get into much trouble), but we certainly developed this relationship as Zach got older. We shared a love of European sports cars and spent hours together tinkering on project cars like my old Saab 900 convertible or his beloved yellow BMW Dakar E36 M3. Once, I went with him to a Saab car show in Pennsylvania. Much to Zach's amusement, I was ill-prepared to sleep in a tent in the middle of a field with hundreds of revving cars and loud young people. I wouldn't have changed a moment of that time shared with him though, creaking joints and all.

We also shared hours watching action-packed or comical movies. "Home Alone" and "Die Hard" were favorite Christmas Eve movies. We shared a love for suspense novels and classic rock, which Zach developed while playing the

Guitar Hero video game. He was also a talented drummer. When he tired of playing in The Maryland Conservatory of Music pop ensemble in favor of an EMO (emotional hardcore) band, I took my earplugs with me to his gigs to survive the auditory assault. Of course, the band practiced at our house, as drums are harder to transport than guitars. Good times.

Zach's love of cars translated into a career at Ford as an auto technician. He got his technician certification and AA degree from a program at a local college. He started working in the Quick Lane doing oil changes and soon became a master mechanic's helper. He obtained many Ford and Automotive Service Excellence (ASC) certifications and was set to become a full-fledged master mechanic. However, his Ford career was short-lived.

Zach loved skateboarding since he was 10 years old and pushed the limits of doing tricks, jumping sets of stairs, or flying off the roof of our shed. His small skateboarding posse decided to start snowboarding in their early twenties. They often hit the trails in the evenings after work. Zach took a bad fall on the last run one night, going off a jump when he was tired, and the mountain was getting icy. Two ligaments in his left shoulder tore and after failing conservative treatment options, he had extensive reconstructive surgery. He was prescribed opiates for his post-op pain control which quickly led to the disease of addiction and frequent treatment programs.

Zach left Ford at age 27 to participate in a nine-month residential recovery program in Florida. He achieved recovery and decided he would remain and live in Florida. His condo in West Palm Beach included a screened porch facing a pond where he liked to sit on his swing and watch the waterfowl. Initially, he worked for an aviation company, building small engine components. Then he decided to leave for a challenging appliance tech position. In October of 2022, he got a fantastic offer from General Electric in the appliance division and was planning on an exciting future with the company.

Zach was never a "social butterfly" or the partying type–preferring to stay home in his condo and read, watch TV, assemble car models, and play video games. He took great care of his condo and his Volkswagen Jetta. He

12 Zach's Dad, Jerry C.

surrounded himself with positive affirmations, such as, his "God is Good" cross and "Don't look back, you aren't going that way" sign. Even his tattoos had meaning. He had the coordinates of our Maryland house on one thigh and a memorial tattoo to a favorite childhood dog, Jessie, on his calf. The leaf pattern on his wrist represented eternity. Just two months prior to passing, Zach got a new tattoo on his other thigh saying "Count Your Blessings" in beautiful cursive script.

While Zach lived in Florida, his mom, Mary Beth, and I continued to live in Maryland. I would fly down to visit Zach every other weekend if schedules permitted. I enjoyed him picking me up at the airport on Friday evening, spending the weekend, and then dropping me off at the airport on Monday morning, so we both could go back to work. We bonded over guy stuff: going to "Cars & Coffee" events, restaurants, movies, hitting golf balls at Drive Shack, and watching YouTube videos. Zach enjoyed showing me around West Palm Beach and Jupiter, Florida. We pondered the future together as we explored the Busch Wildlife Preserve, climbed to the top of Jupiter Lighthouse, or walked the Juno Beach pier. One special memory is the time we saved a group of baby ducks that had fallen into a sewer while the mother duck watched us.

I enjoyed my time with Zach so much that I decided to leave my job in Maryland and accept a position in Florida near Zach's condo. I have great memories of Zach and me driving around trying to find a place for me to live. He was quite a comedian and had many quick-witted comments about the places we toured. In one place in particular, Zach was quick to suggest we just keep driving. "No need to stop the car," Zach said after seeing trash on the sidewalks, old beer cans, and folks just hanging out in the parking lot. When it was his turn to treat us to a meal, he was famous for choosing the COSTCO special—$1.49 for a hotdog and a drink.

My wife, Mary Beth, soon joined me in Florida, and we started to get into a routine that included seeing Zach, mostly on the weekends. We enjoyed going to the beach and pool with Zach or going out for a meal together. We also spent a wonderful week in a beachfront house in Myrtle Beach in August of 2022 with Zach, his brothers Sam and Jake, Sam's wife Megan, Jake's fiancé Lauren, and our little dog Bandit. Zach's aunts, uncle, and cousins were also staying at a house close by. It would be the last time we were all together as a family.

In December, Mary Beth and I had spent a Sunday with Zach, playing pool and making jokes. It was a happy day; I had no suspicions that he was about to relapse. Monday, Zach went to work, and at 9:30 p.m. he texted me to let me know he'd had a great day, made some commissions, and was tired and heading to bed. One explanation for his long day was that he had forgotten a tool at a customer's house and had to drive back there to retrieve it. His text ended with "Love ya, old man." His nightly texts always ended the same way.

Tuesday evening, we hadn't heard from Zach. We drove to his condo, saw his car in his usual spot, and panicked. Mary Beth ran to his door while I parked. She banged on the door as she used her key to open it. The door only opened three inches as the chain lock was fastened. I ran around to the back of the condo to check if I could see anything through the sliding patio door.

I could see Zach on the floor by his lit Christmas tree. I started screaming and ran around to the front door. I shouldered the door until the lock broke off. Then I fell next to my son, and it was obvious that he had already passed away. Rocking back and forth, I continued to scream and cry, all while holding him in my arms.

Emergency Services and the Sheriff's Department arrived and confirmed what I already knew. Mary Beth and I went outside while they processed the scene. We remained there for an hour until the Medical Examiner (ME) arrived to remove Zach's body. Mary Beth and I kept our heads turned away as the ME wheeled the stretcher to the waiting van. We did not want to have that vision ingrained in our minds.

Our suspicions were confirmed four weeks later: Zach had passed from fentanyl poisoning.

The next few weeks after Zach's passing were a painful blur. He passed on December 13, 2022. We had to arrange for a cremation, and somehow make it through the holidays. We had friends from Maryland who spent the time with us in Florida to offer support.

We held a celebration of life for Zach in Maryland in January. We included many items important to Zach: his skateboard, work uniform, tools, Lego car models, artwork, posters, beach chairs, flip-flops, and even pictures of his ultra-organized work van. Reflecting back, Zach's hobbies and meticulous condo and organized work van may have been his attempts to comfort himself and keep his life organized to better deal with the anxiety that was associated with his substance use disorder.

His Florida co-workers and neighbors were not able to attend his celebration of life, but their comments filled my soul with pride and further awareness of the goodness of my son. I was so proud to hear how Zach often helped an elderly lady with her packages and helped another neighbor fix an appliance. One neighbor said, "I always felt safe having Zach around." Zach's boss sent pictures of a group text when he shared the news of Zach's passing with the other appliance techs; "It's just tough. I'm trying to process it. He was an amazing person. Zach was a great guy and excited to be part of our team. Going to miss the guy. Zach was a great kid. Zach was a bright, funny, curious, and very patient guy. I got to know him really well while training him for three weeks. I believed he was going to be a great tech for us. He ran a high-end appliance region, and he wasn't afraid of it. I told him I'd be calling him for help soon. Very eager to learn everything he can with us. So sad for such a thing to happen to him. Will miss our conversations. I'm shocked, very sad. I will miss him. Awesome guy." Family and friends in Maryland echoed these sentiments that Zach was a caring, funny, and smart guy.

His brothers each gave a eulogy. They expressed their pride in their older brother, his mechanical inclination, his humor, and his love for his family, including our dogs, often seen curled up on Zach's lap in pictures. Sam reflected on how Zach had been the best man at his wedding. Zach's best man speech had wedding guests crying with laughter. Jake talked about how he admired Zach's balance and skateboard skills and how he and his friends made skateboard videos titled "Street Sharks." He told the attendees how Zach taught him everything he knows about cars and how they had together torn out the dash to fix the air conditioner, replace the exhaust, and install a lift on Jake's Jeep. Zach would stay out in the garage through heat or cold to finish whatever car project he was working on for himself or others, long after Jake went inside to cool off or warm up. Jake shared how he and Sam always poked fun at Zach about how his "30-minute jobs" would turn into three-plus hours because the older cars never wanted to cooperate.

After the celebration of life, my wife and I had to return to Florida. It was just Mary Beth and I and our little dog, Bandit. We had no family or friends in Florida, which made the coping even harder for us. We were alone–trying to get through each day, heavy with grief and feelings of surrealism. As the first shock started to wane, the trauma set in. Questions loomed. Why did this happen? Did he have anxiety related to job performance or something else? How will our family move forward? Is Zach okay, wherever he is now? Mary Beth and I had been raised believing in God and eternal life, but now we questioned our faith. How could we be assured Zach is in Heaven?

To try to cope, Mary Beth began advocacy work fighting the fentanyl crisis and convincing the government to prevent other families from going through the same tragedy. I returned to work as the CEO of a hospital in Florida. I looked forward to the distraction. But soon I realized that I had returned too early. I had debilitating flashbacks that kept me from functioning in my role. Mary Beth tried to be distracted by her advocacy work, speaking in front of Florida Legislatures, helping plan an awareness event, and setting up a foundation in Zach's memory.

We often went to Maryland to visit family during the first few months. And they visited us in Florida. It was difficult talking with family and friends because we felt life had continued for everyone else, but we had difficulty coping. Mary Beth and I decided to attend individual grief counseling. This seemed to help for a while, as it allowed us to share our feelings with someone else, instead of upsetting each other. Unfortunately, what relief we felt from the counseling was short-lived, and within a day after each session, we were back to being miserable.

We realized that not having family or friends nearby had a negative impact on our healing. We texted often but had phone calls less frequently. It was the in-person contact and support that we needed. My co-workers seemed hesitant to discuss my situation, but I was able to connect with someone who went through something similar.

Mary Beth and I avoided the news, and we rarely watched a current television show. Instead, we stuck to old classics, where there is less drama or controversy. To us, this was helpful and may have had a healing effect.

Around two months after Zach's passing, Mary Beth began researching mediums. We wanted confirmation that our Zach was fine. We needed something to help us cope. I had had only one dream visitation from Zach. He was standing in front of me nodding his head and saying, "Oh yeah, I am okay." I wanted more evidence. Mary Beth found a medium that came highly recommended. I was apprehensive and borderline skeptical but was hopeful that this would help to decrease our worries and assure us that even though Zach was not physically here, he was still present.

One night, I was preparing to go to work for an evening meeting, and Mary Beth was logging on for her session with the medium. She retreated to the bedroom, and I was in the living room gathering my supplies for the meeting. I could hear Mary Beth talking via the Zoom connection, and I could also hear a man's voice on the speaker, but I could not make out what he was saying. I had to leave soon, so I placed my ear against the door to listen. I could hear "Popcorn popcorn popcorn, why is he so animated about showing me popcorn?" The medium was getting this from Zach. Mary Beth said, "Not sure, but Zach liked popcorn." They continued to talk, and I left.

Our parking spaces were on the same floor as our condo. I could walk through a couple of doors directly into the garage to our two assigned spaces. When I reached our spots, I noticed a couple of items on the garage floor between our cars: two puffed kernels of popcorn. I started to cry. I searched the area; no other popcorn was found. Right then, I realized why the medium was stressing how Zach was telling him about popcorn. It was Zach letting me know he was okay. Had I not somehow gotten the message from Zach, I never would have understood the relevance of these two little popped kernels between our cars.

Through the medium, Mary Beth found a support group called "Helping Parents Heal." She watched their Zoom sessions and YouTube videos and read many books that the presenters recommended. This was a major difference-maker as she identified with their non-dogmatic view of the afterlife. Through HPH, Mary Beth heard about a fathers' group; Helping Fathers Heal. I began attending this group five months after Zach's passing and found this was a game-changer for me. Although I didn't often speak during the Zoom group meetings, listening to what others were doing on their grief journeys helped me realize I was not alone.

I have learned that life will never be the same. The finality of Zach's passing sinks in more each day. Just nine months after his transition and I still cry every day, but I try to remember all the great times that I shared with him. Often, I cry in the car as I drive by one of the restaurants or stores we used to visit. I have not turned on the radio in the car since his passing, as I fear I may hear a song that triggers an emotional outbreak. Many times, while at work, I had to excuse myself from meetings or close the door to my office because my emotions were taking over.

The only thing to do was to take a leave of absence from work and consult a professional. Post Traumatic Stress Disorder (PTSD) is real, and the flashbacks from December 13th were not allowing me to function. I found that it was okay to admit I needed help, and with the help of my physician, I found a medication that would limit my flashbacks, moderate my emotions, and allow me to return to work after five weeks. As a health professional, I was surprised that I hadn't asked for help earlier; I wish I had. The grieving process made me realize just how much I loved my son. The old saying, "You never know how much you love something until it is no longer there," is putting it mildly.

The grief journey is not the same for all of us. We each grieve differently. One way is no better or worse than another. I look at and listen to others talk about their grief and I wonder, "How do they go on?" Some fathers seem to have it more together than others. I am open to other's suggestions, but I don't always expect the same results. I'll just keep doing what works for me.

I haven't found "the answer" to combating grief; an answer may not exist. Talking to others going through the same thing helps, as well as sharing positive memories of my son. My frequent walks have helped me, too. Mary Beth and I, at the eleventh-month mark, are only just beginning to do some of the things we used to enjoy. Starting slowly by going out to an occasional dinner, sitting by the water's edge, and taking drives. These things sound simplistic, but they remain very hard for us to do. I feel a pang of guilt if I am laughing at something, or not thinking of Zach. I then ask myself, "What would Zach want?" I know that he would not want his mom or me to suffer or feel guilty; that would upset him terribly. Zach would also support our recent decision to move back to Maryland to live closer to his brothers and the rest of our family.

I talk to Zach daily…I touch his money tree, which he purchased shortly before landing his GE job. Maybe I will try meditation like my wife has been doing to still my mind. If I can find that in-between space, perhaps I can make a stronger connection with Zach in spirit. Through it all, I am now a firm believer that while my son is no longer physically here, he is "fine," and I look forward to the day I get to see and hold him again.

13 Miles' Dad, David K.

How do I sum up Miles? It's very difficult for me to express these precious memories because of the emotions the memories bring back. But I want you to know Miles' impact, in the sincere hope that his memory will continue. No parent wants their child to be forgotten.

Miles is our third of four children and was born on a cold, damp morning in Pittsburgh, PA on May 26, 1996. Miles was the type of person everyone would want their child to be: respectful; polite; genuine; caring; and intelligent. Any positive adjective...that was Miles. We heard this from parents and teachers alike. One of my favorites is "exuberant", which is how a friend of ours described Miles when he was five. Miles was also joyful and loved to laugh.

Friends were always special to Miles and there was rarely a time when he wasn't surrounded by a group of kids–whether it be classmates, or teammates from soccer, football, track, or cross country. Laughter and joy were a constant with Miles, which allowed him to make friends very easily. These friendships were very important to him, and he worked hard to be inclusive with everyone.

Because Miles was always surrounded by friends and was an excellent student, we never worried about him–even when he surprisingly didn't get into the engineering program at Purdue (a dream of his since he was six). We certainly knew this was a blow to Miles, but we thought he would shake it off. So, when his mood started to change, it was easy to attribute it to "just being a teenager." The mood swings would happen, but I would think to myself, "Miles is such a happy person–nothing will keep him down." Miles ended up going to the University of Detroit Mercy where he had a few friends from high school, then made a bunch of new friends on the cross country and track teams.

However, even with good grades and lots of friends, Miles started having darker periods and was hospitalized a couple of times for suicidal thoughts. Miles' grandfather passed away during the second semester of Miles's junior year at Detroit Mercy. He was very close to his grandfather. Two weeks later, Miles called me and admitted that he needed to drop out so he could enter an extended treatment program. I immediately left work and drove the three hours to pick him up. I can still remember standing in the driveway of his apartment, holding him tightly and letting him know that I loved him and that we would get through this.

After several weeks, we were able to get Miles into an extended program at an excellent treatment facility in Atlanta. This would allow him to work on

13 Miles' Dad, David K.

his anxiety and depression. After his stay, we believed that Miles was strong enough to go back to Detroit Mercy and finish his senior year, so he returned and seemed to pick up where he left off: lots of friends and good grades.

Miles and I had a good relationship and we loved talking with each other. However, I wouldn't say that we were terribly close, like when you hear people say, "My child is my best friend." I regret that we did not have a relationship where we could share our inner feelings. I am sure that Miles learned this from me, as I struggle with sharing my own feelings.

My fondest memories of Miles were of the times that we ran together. This began when he was very young and sitting in a jogging stroller and continued as he grew older. My favorite run with Miles was when he was nineteen, during a family vacation in Beijing, China. It was a great vacation, and we had all four children together. During this incredible trip, Miles and I made a point of running together for a couple of days. This special run happened when we got up at 4:30 in the morning. The route took us through Tiananmen Square, where we were the only Westerners among tens of thousands of Chinese who were there to take part in the flag-raising ceremony. This is such an incredibly special memory for me. I take this photo with me wherever I go.

I'll share another fun story that always makes me smile because it's so typical of Miles' style. Miles had a very good friend, Grace, who was competing in the Miss Indiana competition, and she invited him for the weekend as her escort. Throughout the event, Miles kept asking Grace to introduce him to the other contestants and to get their numbers for him. Hearing Grace tell the story always cracks me up.

Miles passed by suicide on April 27, 2019. We do not say he committed suicide because that word implies that he perpetrated the act. This is a day that will forever be the worst day of our lives. It is still too painful for me to go into the details, but this was the day that Miles took his final college exam in order to graduate with a degree in Robotics and Mechatronic System Engineering. We will never know what was on Miles' mind that evening. We can only assume that maybe he felt his exams did not go well and that he was a failure because he did not yet have a glamorous, high-paying job like his friends. We were woken up that morning by a call that no parent should have to receive.

We were invited to take part in the graduation ceremonies and the school officials were very gentle and kind to us. We even walked in the ceremony and picked up Miles' diploma when his name was called. Needless to say, this was an extremely difficult task, but one we felt drawn to do. We even received a five-minute standing ovation from the crowd and too many hugs to count from Miles' classmates. However, I continue to be confused as to why there is an asterisk next to Miles' name in the graduation program. It states that the diploma was awarded "posthumously." Miles completed and passed all his classes, so to me, there should be no special notation. Additionally, Miles' diploma states that it was awarded on April 27, 2019, which was the day he passed. Other diplomas show the date of the actual graduation ceremony. These modifications highlight the tragic circumstances of the graduation, and it hurts.

The first few months were a blur, and I was in complete disbelief. We knew Miles had mental health issues, but we thought he was headed in a positive direction. We had no idea it would come to him taking his own life to end his pain. I still regret going back to work after less than two weeks, even though I was told that I did not have to return so quickly. I think I just didn't know what else to do. We didn't want to go out of the house or interact with others because we felt that we were always being looked at with pity and did not know what to say when approached.

Miles passed away on a Saturday. Since we had no family living locally, we scheduled his visitation and service for the following Friday and Saturday. The number of friends and family that came to support us was incredible. Several of his school professors and administrators drove the three hours from Detroit to join us. Many friends from the Atlanta treatment facility, as well as classmates and team members from cross country and track attended. We had so many people at our house throughout that weekend. However, my wife, Lisa, did not want anyone sitting in Miles' chair at the table, so she placed a big picture of him in the seat. More than four years later that picture is still there joining us for all our meals.

I remember the fear of wondering what would happen to Lisa and our family. It's understandable because Lisa was a wreck, just like me. However, we committed to each other that we would find a way to support one another as best we could. We've all heard the statistics of the high divorce rate among parents who have suffered the passing of their child. I recall looking it up once and seeing numbers as high as 80%, which really scared me. I have since seen the numbers are much lower. Regardless, we already lost a child–we were not going to lose each other, or our other children!

Setting a path to our new normal was also a concern. I really do not know what we did most of that time, but I do recall the first Friday night after Miles passed. Lisa and I watched a movie at home. It felt odd that we were trying to do something "normal." Many parents question if they will ever laugh again or feel happiness. For several months, any laughter created a great deal of guilt. The feelings of guilt do go away, and you will laugh and feel happiness again. However, in my experience, the highs are never as high or as long and the lows are lower or even longer – just a fact I've had to deal with.

Where did we find support? Other than the support groups that I will address later, we've found support in each other and with family. The support can come in many forms: from actively discussing feelings and emotions, to including Miles in conversations. Our immediate and extended families have never avoided a conversation that would include Miles, which helps us know that he has not been forgotten. The stories and laughter about Miles are so casual and natural that they bring a great deal of comfort.

I think perhaps that I am not a good griever (if there is such a thing). I typically compartmentalize my feelings. I truly do not know what I have learned from all this, other than to say I believe I am more empathetic. Sometimes, I think I'm sympathetic. At other times, I am completely numb. I have asked myself hundreds of times, where do I go from here?

What has surprised me? The biggest surprise is how random and raw my emotions can still be after four-plus years, and that the emotions can flair up anytime, making me just melt. The number of things I see or hear that remind me of Miles is still shocking. To be sure, many random things remind me of my other children. However, I still carry the raw emotion I experience from thoughts of Miles. As I was leaving the grocery store a couple of days ago, there was a mother and her son selling Cub Scout popcorn in the store lobby. It brought back a flood of memories from when I was Miles' Cub Scout leader from the same Pack, and I helped him sell popcorn. Fun memories of twenty years ago, but the tears just flowed on the drive home.

Advice for other fathers? Don't be too hard on yourself, and let your emotions take you where they will. To me, there is an emotional side and there is an intellectual side. The emotional side will tell you that you should have done more. It makes you question every action that you did, or did not, take. You question why you said this but not that, why didn't you listen more or why you didn't spend more time with your child, and why didn't you take more pictures and videos so you could see his face and hear his voice. The list is endless. You beat yourself up constantly. The intellectual side tries to convince you that you did your best. Spoiler alert: the intellectual side rarely wins.

Additionally, finding a support group can be helpful. There are online communities that have local chapter affiliates, be it a Compassionate Friends-type organization or Helping Parents Heal (HPH), with its affiliate for the dads, Helping Fathers Heal (HFH). It is important to know that there are others going through the same thing and they will be there for you. Even if you do not actively participate, it can be beneficial and reassuring to listen.

Finally, do not let anger and bitterness win and take over. Many people can be angry at their loved one for choosing to end their life or for the circumstances that led to their passing, or angry at friends and family for saying the wrong thing, or worse, not saying anything at all. I refuse to be angry at Miles. Instead, I am incredibly sad that he felt there was no hope left, or that he could not trust his mom and me enough to share his troubles with us. Miles passed because of an illness, only this was a mental illness, not a physical illness.

The most helpful practice for my own healing includes being a part of

13 Miles' Dad, David K.

a group of parents who have lost a child as well. I find it very reassuring to hear their experiences and then to be able to relate them back to my own journey. I am in two groups: a support group specific to suicide and Helping Fathers Heal. Each has its own benefits, however, I relate most to the father's group. While I am not an "active" participant and typically do not verbally contribute (there are many fathers like me on our weekly video call who are passive participants), I truly look forward to our Wednesday evening Zoom calls.

I am also a very active triathlete, which has been a passion of mine for many years. This is something I have made a conscious effort to continue. It is a great stress reliever and also ensures that I get out with training partners to just do my own thing. Each time Miles' birthday comes around, or the anniversary of his passing, I go for a long run on a route we used to do together. So, I would suggest finding a hobby or activity that is physically and mentally healthy and gives you an opportunity to be yourself.

Have I seen signs? I wish that I could definitively say "yes", but I just do not know. I recall bringing up in HFH that I wish I could have a sign from Miles. One of the fathers who regularly has signs from his son told me that I should verbally ask Miles for a sign and be very specific. I have not received responses to my specific asks, but I do attribute certain events or sightings to Miles and immediately think of him: a cardinal, a rainbow, even a shirtless, skinny runner...all will make me instantly think of my son.

Experiences with mediums and visitations? After thinking about it for four years, my wife and I finally had a reading with a medium recommended by HPH. We both went into the reading not knowing what to expect but had open minds. I invited two of our adult children to join us if they were interested. However, they had no interest in participating. They probably think we are crazy, but as I said to one daughter, "I will make no excuses or apologies for anything I do as it relates to Miles." That translates to "I am desperate for any sign from Miles, so do not question this."

The reading went well, but there was nothing that specifically came out of it that just blew us away or that we could directly attribute to Miles. There were a few things that were spot on, but then some that felt like the medium was fumbling. In the end, the medium told us that Miles loves us and does not want us to be hard on ourselves. Maybe I am too pragmatic, but I would not expect anything different. Bottom line, there was nothing that would make me call "bunk" on this medium. My wife and I are in agreement that we will try again.

As for dreams, in the past four years, I am sure that I have had less than five dreams that I can remember but, just as with signs, I am envious of those fathers that have them. I just wish they would come more often. One of the few dreams about Miles that I do vividly recall happened about a year after he passed. I dreamt that I was at a party telling others about my family. When I got to Miles, I had to say, "But he passed away." It was awful and I still feel how traumatic it was waking up and just sobbing uncontrollably. It continues to bring tears to my eyes after more than three years.

How would I sum this up?

Please NEVER STOP TALKING ABOUT MY SON. You can ask me questions or bring up memories of Miles–every one of them is treasured and I can assure you that I remember every time someone randomly approached me to offer a kind gesture or words of encouragement. My first time returning to the gym after Miles passed, one person walked by me while on the treadmill and gave me a fist bump and another walked past me as I was shaving and just patted my shoulder and nodded. Nothing was said, but these were extremely meaningful gestures to me since they were letting me know that they cared. Conversely, I remember every person who has completely ignored Miles' passing. My friends know that I bring up stories about Miles in everyday conversation and treat those stories just as I would stories about my other children. I believe that in doing so, I am showing others that it is okay to bring up Miles, and I am keeping his memory alive.

Finally, let me share a pet peeve: please do not ask what my son's name was. My son's name *is* Miles, not *was* Miles. I had four children prior to Miles passing away and I still have four children now; one is just in heaven. He will always be my son and I will always love him. I am not only proud of him but

13 Miles' Dad, David K.

proud to be his father. I love you Miles Scott Kelleher and I miss you more than you will ever know.

14 Dylan's Dad, Mike E.

Every human being experiences loss at one time or another. In my opinion, the worst possible trauma a human being can experience is the passing of one's child. I will never "get over" missing Dylan's physical presence, but my experiences have proven he still exists and is thriving. It's comforting to know that he is only one thought away from being with me.

My ex-wife and I got married in our early 30's, and we each had a career. After a couple of years, we decided it was time to have a child. After three years we gave up and–as with so many others–that's when Allyson got pregnant. Dylan was born on October 21, 1992. I realize I'm biased, but he was gifted in many ways. Dylan was the "perfect son" growing up–caring, empathetic, intelligent, handsome, and very loving.

In 1994 I accepted a transfer to Singapore. We decided it would be a good life experience for the three of us, and it was. We lived in Singapore, then transferred to Perth in Western Australia. Our last move was to Jakarta, Indonesia. Together we were in the Asia-Pacific area for about ten years, and we shared many incredible experiences.

We moved back to Katy, Texas in 2003 and Dylan entered middle school. It was there that he discovered a passion for music. Dylan wanted to play drums, but there were no openings, so he played trumpet for a year. The next year he took up the drums and soon became a very accomplished percussionist. Dylan was the first percussionist from his high school to make it to State competitions and did so three years in a row. Dylan also discovered a competitive Drum Corps organization based in the northeast. He played the quad drums in his marching bands for three summers straight. So, his sophomore, junior, and senior years were very active.

At age fifteen, Dylan began to change, becoming more combative and argumentative with us. I realize it's typical for many teens, but Dylan's change was more drastic than many others. He began to dabble in drinking, smoking pot, and experimenting with Xanax and other drugs. Despite his high intelligence, his grades became mediocre. Drum Corps are run in a very strict manner with zero tolerance for drugs or drinking. Dylan loved it so much, he would stay sober during those three summers. When he returned home after each season, he would resume his drug usage.

Dylan was offered a full scholarship to Baylor as a music major. He knew many others who had taken that path and became music teachers. Dylan didn't want that path, so he opted to go to Texas Christian University (TCU) for business. He went directly from his senior year in Drum Corps to TCU, and he fell in with the wrong crowd almost as soon as he got to Fort Worth. He lasted only two semesters due to drugs. Dylan was an addict who was attracted to anything that made him feel different or better.

When Dylan left TCU in 2011, he eventually went to work for a

14 Dylan's Dad, Mike E.

company in Austin. He had a motorcycle accident and the doctors prescribed opioids for the pain. It didn't take long for Dylan to abuse the drug and become addicted. When they were no longer available, a business acquaintance introduced Dylan to heroin. His addiction only got worse, and it wasn't long before he was injecting the poison. Dylan self-medicated with heroin for around five years. He went to various treatment centers, totaled five cars, began to steal to fund his habit, and lost our trust during those years, not to mention the negative physical and mental effects.

In the spring of 2016, Dylan was arrested for possession and forced to detox (painfully) in the county jail. His life was now completely unravelling so he entered himself into his third and final treatment center on his own. I was so proud of him. This time the treatment was effective, and Dylan stayed sober for six months.

During those six months, we were very blessed to have the "real" Dylan back! He was very active in youth Alcoholics Anonymous groups, training at CrossFit, eating healthy, and back into the best shape of his life.

After months of sobriety, Dylan took another job in Austin, working for a wedding catering service. Dylan also decided to enroll in Lone Star Junior College in Houston to get his Licensed Chemical Dependency Certification (LCDC) to help other addicts recover. He would return to stay with us on Sunday, Monday, and Tuesday nights so he could attend the classes.

Thanksgiving of 2016 was my best and worst ever. We had a great time with Dylan and his new girlfriend. They worked together, so they returned to Austin that Friday. During his drive back to Katy two days later, he saw his heroin dealer. On Monday afternoon, Allyson returned from running errands and found Dylan on the couch, sounding, and acting normal but complaining of stomach pain. He went back to his bedroom at around 4:30.

I returned home from work around 4:50. Allyson came to me, saying she couldn't get Dylan up. I gave him CPR for around 20 minutes, while Allyson waited on Emergency Medical Services. I never managed to get his heart going again, but EMS did. At the hospital, we were told his brain had swelled from the lack of oxygen, and he was brain dead. Almost exactly a day after we found him, his body gave out with a heart attack. We'll never know why Dylan decided to relapse, but his body had gotten healthy and no longer had a tolerance for heroin.

When Dylan passed, I "intellectualized" my grief. My mission became finding irrefutable evidence that our son was in a good place and thriving. I didn't want anyone to tell me where Dylan was. I wanted to know "my truth" and get it firsthand. I read everything I could get my hands on: Near Death Experiences (NDEs), Out of Body Experiences (OBEs), Astral Travel, Mediumship, and more.

The signs I've received from Dylan are too numerous to share, but the following are examples of the most significant:

1) Dylan passed away in November 2016. The month before, I asked what he wanted for Christmas since he was doing so well. He chose a specific brand of watch. I ordered the watch, and it coincidentally arrived the day after Dylan's service. We had forgotten about it.

I researched local mediums and our first reading with Dylan was July 1, 2017. Towards the end of this very accurate reading, our medium said, "Dylan wants me to tell you that he's sorry about the watch."

2) I had a habit of talking to Dylan in the car. Once, I was staying at our place in Estes Park, Colorado, and talking to Dylan as I ran some errands. Now, it's a fact that I'm a Diet Coke-aholic, and Dylan used to give me a hard time about how bad they were for me. I pulled into a convenience store to buy one. This was during the time when Coke was putting names on the back of their plastic bottles as a marketing effort. I walked up to the Coke display, and all but one bottle was facing forward. I grabbed that one...and on the back, it said "Dad."

3) I was on my way to work on January 23, 2018, and giving Dylan a hard time, as usual. I thanked him for his signs to date but challenged him to come up with something that couldn't be refuted.

The next day, Allyson and I came home from a YMCA workout and we each took showers. During Allyson's shower, she discovered a small, pink opal on the shower floor, so flawed it couldn't have been from jewelry. It was Dylan's birthstone. I showed the stone to a favorite medium and asked what it was. She nonchalantly said, "It's an apport, a manifestation from the other side." I asked, "What am I supposed to do with it"? She replied, "Just be grateful" and to know that Dylan most likely couldn't have done it on his own. I Googled the meaning of pink opals to discover that most are associated with unconscious pain.

Pink opal manifests as a pink color that is supposed to help you recognize old wounds, anger, and fear in order to heal successfully. It helps the healing process to dissolve painful memories with gentleness and the sacredness of compassion.

When Dylan "went home" I wondered how the rest of the world could continue to function—what was wrong with these people?! And some of the comments were insensitive. For anyone reading this who has not experienced the passing of their own child, please realize we're very vulnerable, especially in the early, traumatic days. I call it being in the Fog.

A couple of things NOT to say to a parent who's just lost a child:

"Dylan's in a better place now."

"It's been four months, so now you can begin to move on."

Studies show that four months is the typical "grace period" others expect before we go back to a normal life, whatever that's supposed to look like after this happens to you. Of course, all these comments come from people without any direct experience, so I've learned to forgive their insensitivity...most of the time.

Soon after Dylan passed, I had lunch with a man I had worked with for more than 20 years. During our conversation, he said, "I'd never let one of my kids get addicted. I'd cuff them to their beds before I'd let that happen." This is my most extreme example of insensitivity and I still find it unbelievable. I stood up and left him with the bill.

My Advice for Bereaved Parents:

1. There are no rules or timelines for grief. Each parent needs to realize they will experience different stages of grief at different times.

2. I strongly recommend that spouses and siblings meet regularly to specifically ask what the other(s) need from them by way of support. The caring and love will be reciprocated if done with sincerity and regularity.

3. Live forward and learn backward. Be in the moment but learn from your experiences.

4. We are exactly where we should be at any point in time, good or bad. We may not like where we are, but we need to learn from our experiences, no matter what.

5. Things happen exactly the way they're supposed to, and we don't have to understand why. I spent months feeling guilty about being a father who hadn't protected his family. That was my job! After I let go of the guilt and came to believe I wasn't in control of the situation, a huge weight was lifted from my shoulders, and I began to heal.

6. Triggers are people, places, or things that can bring back negative memories. I call it "replaying the tapes" of our negative experiences, including the actual passing of our child. Quick examples–driving by Dylan's middle and high schools, going to one of his favorite restaurants, walking down the grocery aisle and seeing Dylan's favorite cereals, watching a favorite movie, or listening to a favorite band we both enjoyed.

7. I have learned to store three of my favorite memories with Dylan in my hip pocket. When I start to replay how Dylan passed and the history of his drug abuse, I replace it with one or all of those great memories. With patience, awareness, perseverance, and time, it can result in immediate relief.

8. I'm going to do my best to live the rest of my life in a manner that will make Dylan proud of me.

9. Above all else, acceptance and patience are the keys to realizing we don't have to understand the reason for what has happened. Once I embraced this, I finally began to heal.

In conclusion, Dylan's story is one of resilience, recovery, and the enduring power of love. Despite the challenges he faced, his legacy inspires me to live a life that would make him proud when we reunite. Acceptance and patience have been my greatest allies in the healing process, allowing me to find peace amidst the pain. I wish the same for all other parents who've shared this experience.

15 Austin's Dad, Jeff C.

    Our beloved first son, Austin Gilbert Cottrell, was born on November 29, 1995. My wife Nan and I marveled at the sight of our beautiful baby boy. Austin's middle name was a tribute to my late grandfather, a truly compassionate and selfless individual. Austin showed those same qualities from an early age.

    Austin's brother, Kevin, was born in 1997, and his sister Baylee in 2002. We prioritized family time. We loved playing card games unique to Wisconsin, such as Sheepshead, Cribbage, and Smear. We thrived in the outdoors. At our cabin on Great Bass Lake–in the serene forests of northern Wisconsin–we fished, swam, kayaked, and hiked. In that serene setting, free of television, we forged precious memories and strengthened our bond.

As he grew, Austin explored sports, including soccer, baseball, basketball, and football. He hated to lose, and his hyper-competitiveness showed up whether you were playing a board game or competing on the court or the field.

Austin also loved to sing and perform. He listened to music all the time. He learned the piano at the age of seven and had an amazing ability to memorize music. We never figured out if it was finger-memory or photographic memory. Once he performed a piece of music, he never had to look at the sheet music again. From early childhood to his teenage years, he would often belt out the "Star-Spangled Banner" from the shower at the top of his lungs. We just shook our heads and grinned.

When he organized games, Austin always made sure that everyone participated. This caring and inclusive nature was one of his best qualities. One particular memory stands out. During his time in middle school, Nan noticed that Austin would come home hungry every day. She discovered that he had been giving away the lunch she packed for him to children who had very little. Austin wanted to ensure that others had enough to eat. In response, Nan started packing him two lunches. Despite this, he would still return home hungry, having shared double the amount of food with his classmates.

During his basketball years as a freshman and sophomore in high school, Austin spent more time on the bench than on the court. But he showed unwavering dedication during practice and supported his teammates wholeheartedly. As a reward for Austin's sportsmanship and selflessness, during the last game of the season, the coach put him in the starting lineup. It was a proud moment for Austin. At the season's awards banquet, the coach's words resonated deeply, "The best compliment I can give is that I have a son, and when he grows up, I want him to be just like Austin Cottrell."

His love for music and performing bloomed in his teenage years. He and his fellow performers would often gather at our house, making use of the pool and spending teenage time in the basement room we had set up for them.

15 Austin's Dad, Jeff C.

Unexpectedly, they would break into impromptu a cappella songs, sometimes even performing barbershop quartet pieces. The sound would fill our home, and as far as we were concerned, they could go on like that all night. Austin took part in numerous musical groups and theater productions, including a memorable rendition of "Sweeney Todd" during his college years.

Austin went on to pursue a degree in finance and economics in college. His memory always astonished everyone. In his younger years, when he received a Harry Potter book, he would disappear into his room, devouring it, and then provide us with intricate details. In college, he and Kevin had the same finance class. Kevin would diligently focus on the lectures, taking meticulous notes, while Austin would research sports statistics on his iPhone. However, whenever the professor called on him, Austin would casually glance up from his phone and provide the correct answer. His friends later confessed that–without Austin's help–they would have struggled to navigate their finance and economics classes.

After graduation, Austin dreamed of working for Vanguard, an investment brokerage firm in Scottsdale, Arizona. He applied and received a job offer from them. He wanted to become a Certified Financial Planner. He chose Vanguard because it was the most ethical company. In March of 2019, we helped him move from Oshkosh, WI to Scottsdale. He was relishing his independence, settling into his own apartment, and buying his first car, a white Ford Fusion. He was set to dive into his career, and excited for what his independence would bring. Little did we know how tragically short his life would be.

In December 2019, our middle child, Kevin, graduated from college, and Austin eagerly looked forward to the ceremony back home in Wisconsin. After celebrating with family and friends at our house, Austin wanted to hit the campus bars with his friends. We made sure everyone had a ride home. Austin planned to stay overnight with friends in off-campus housing, using Uber to get around. That night, however, it all went tragically wrong.

Tired from a long day of travel and celebration, Austin changed plans around midnight and decided to get a ride home, rather than stay out with his friends. We had recently moved to a new house in a more rural setting, just before Austin relocated to Scottsdale. So, he was not very familiar with the new area. The Uber driver brought Austin to our neighborhood but turned down the wrong street and dropped him off at the wrong house. Austin knocked, but the residents at that house did not let him in. They called the police and told Austin to wait outside. Austin called the Uber driver back, was picked up and–unbelievably–dropped off in another unfamiliar part of our development. Confused and frustrated, Austin called for another Uber. But before the driver could reach him, his phone's battery died due to the cold weather.

Austin was left with no other choice and set out on foot, trying to flag down passing cars or get help from various houses. He ended up in a different neighborhood, four miles from our house, knocking on a final door in the early hours of the morning. The resident was a woman, scared and alone in her home. She called the police, but by the time they arrived, Austin had already moved on.

The following morning, I had to go to work for a few hours. Upon finishing, I texted Austin to see if he needed a ride but received no response. Worried, I contacted Kevin, who told me that Austin had returned home the previous night. Panic set in. I called Nan to see if Austin had come home without our knowledge. He hadn't. So, at that point, we were both panicking. We called the police and, based on reports they received from neighbors, we confirmed that it was Austin who was lost and looking for help the night before. The police and fire departments and volunteers searched all day and into the night until it got too cold, and the police halted the search until morning. Our last hopes for a good outcome were destroyed the next morning. They found Austin's body. Lost and confused, he had passed from hypothermia.

Our lives were shattered. How could this happen? Our vibrant 24-year-old son, bursting with potential, was taken from us without warning or the chance to say goodbye. It felt surreal, as if we were trapped in a never-ending nightmare. In the months following his passing, we existed on autopilot. We

15 Austin's Dad, Jeff C.

somehow managed to plan his memorial service. We traveled to Arizona to handle his belongings. Somehow, we fulfilled our daily responsibilities, despite the overwhelming grief.

Initially, we received an outpouring of support from family, friends, and our community. As time passed, this support tapered off, leaving only a few cherished friends who continued to check in on us and offer listening ears. It was incredibly difficult to see life moving forward when we were still grappling with the loss. Our lives were forever changed, and we had to adapt to a new normal.

In our search for healing, Nan, an avid reader, delved into books that explored the experiences of others who had traveled the grief path. She also sought solace in videos and documentaries that touched on the afterlife. Through her research, we discovered invaluable sources of healing.

One of the books Nan recommended was "My Search for Christopher on The Other Side" by Joe McQuillen. This book captivated me, as McQuillen's son had also tragically passed away in cold weather in Wisconsin. Among other things, McQuillen's book covered stories of mediums. I had been skeptical about mediums, but the possibility of communicating with our departed children intrigued me.

Later that winter, we took a short trip to Las Vegas to escape the cold weather. We had to change hotels at the last minute, and it proved to be a true synchronicity. During the taxi ride to our new hotel, we spotted an ad for a medium–the very same medium mentioned in McQuillen's book. This medium happened to be performing at our hotel, the one we decided to change to. We looked into tickets; only two remained, another "divine intervention." We booked the tickets and attended the show.

That evening, during the medium's gallery readings, Austin came through loud and clear. The medium relayed many detailed messages from him: a young man, 24 years old; who had recently passed away in an accident; and who referred to the overwhelming turnout at his memorial service. It was our first experience with a medium. We were sure he had connected with Austin. Any remaining skepticism I had evaporated, and we were hungry for more.

Another resource Nan discovered was Craig McMahon's "Life to Afterlife" Spirituality Series of documentaries. We watched parents talk about their grief journey and share stories of their connections with their children in Spirit. This motivated us to explore more avenues that could help us connect with Austin. During this exploration, we stumbled upon Helping Parents Heal (HPH), an organization that offered invaluable support and resources during our darkest hours.

Despite finding these sources of comfort, we were still in the early stages of grief, grappling with the physical and emotional pain that left us exhausted. This intense anguish was a pain I had never felt before; my entire body hurt, and I found it difficult to concentrate on anything. I was surprised so many everyday things would trigger a deep sense of grief and longing to have my son back by my side. A song on the radio or a memory resurfacing on social media could unleash the emotional floodgates. Grief brings with it a wide range of reactions, from anger and guilt to denial and numbness. I couldn't make sense of all the emotions I was feeling.

Another source of support was finding the HPH affiliate group, Helping Father's Heal. At my first Zoom meeting, I was unable to speak, so I just listened to other dads share their stories and talk about their children who had passed. I realized that this was a brotherhood and a safe place to talk about grief with other men who truly understood what I was going through. A place where I could ask questions and get new perspectives about my grief journey as well as talk about afterlife evidence. This was a place where I could talk about Austin without making anyone else feel uncomfortable. As I grew more confident, I began sharing signs and messages we had received from Austin. I'd like to share some of those signs.

One TV show our family watched was 'Criminal Minds'. I mentioned earlier that Austin's memory was second to none. He could identify which season and episode number was on screen shortly after it started. When we challenged him, he was always proven right. Each episode ended with a recital of a famous quote. At Austin's memorial service, Nan, and I, along with our

15 Austin's Dad, Jeff C.

children, spoke to honor Austin. Fittingly, Nan concluded the final eulogy with a quote from the show about the sacredness of tears. She finished by saying, "From Season Five, Episode 11," for Austin. A week later, our family was at home, and we decided to watch an episode of Criminal Minds, for Austin. Our television hadn't been on for weeks, and we turned it on and opened Netflix. Without selecting anything, Season Five, Episode 11 started playing. We just looked at each other wondering how that was possible.

Another sign we received early on was a message from someone who attended the memorial service. During my eulogy, I challenged everyone at the service to try and make something good come from this tragedy and asked them to perform a random act of kindness in memory of Austin. Weeks after the service, a couple in their car saw a young man walking and struggling to carry his groceries. As they drove by, they remembered the request for a random act of kindness. They turned around and offered a ride to the young man. As they chatted, they asked the young man what his name was. He replied, "Austin".

Recently, I was at my other son, Kevin's wedding, and went down to the water's edge to watch the sunrise and reflect on the day ahead of us. I talked to Austin, telling him how much I miss him and wanted him to be part of this special day. I asked him for a sign and soon after I gazed up to the sky and saw two clouds next to each other each shaped as a vertical line, forming the number 11. Eleven is a significant number for our family and I knew it was from him. Austin and I were both born in November, the eleventh month, and 11 was always my choice for a jersey number in any sport I played. The kids would try to get number 11 if they could. We all put 11 in passwords and screennames, as well.

We have had several readings from amazing mediums who connected with Austin and have given us undeniable evidence that he is still present in our lives. At one medium reading, he was even able to spoil a surprise gift for his sister. My wife, Nan, and our daughter, Baylee, took part with me. We had bought Baylee diamond earrings as a surprise gift for her high school graduation. The medium repeatedly asked us about "the earrings" until we finally had to tell Baylee about her gift, just so she was aware of what was happening. Austin was always the "secret spoiler" for all manner of surprises. We knew it was him in his mischievous way.

In our most recent reading, the medium picked up on Austin's kindness and wanting to help others who weren't as fortunate. The medium said to Nan, "Austin would ask you to pack him an extra lunch, wouldn't he?" and if you recall the story earlier in this chapter about Austin giving his lunches away it was clearly a message from him. Knowing that Austin is still present in our lives gives us comfort and we know we will be reunited with him one day.

For other dads reading this, my advice to you is to reach out for help in whatever form you're comfortable with. Do not try to 'go it alone'. Don't internalize your grief. Find those special people you are comfortable with and talk through your feelings and talk about your child(ren). Keep your child(ren) present in your life, and with time and support, you will begin to take control of your grief rather than have your grief control you. You can do it, and just know there are many dads on the same journey who are willing to help. Helping Fathers Heal is a unique resource, where you can connect with other dads who understand and can offer help and guidance along your grief journey. We can honor our kids by healing and helping others and they will be by our side, helping us every step of the way.

Dedicated to my son Austin Cottrell – I love you so much, son. You continue to inspire me, and I am so proud to be your Dad!

16 Lexi's Dad, Matt G.

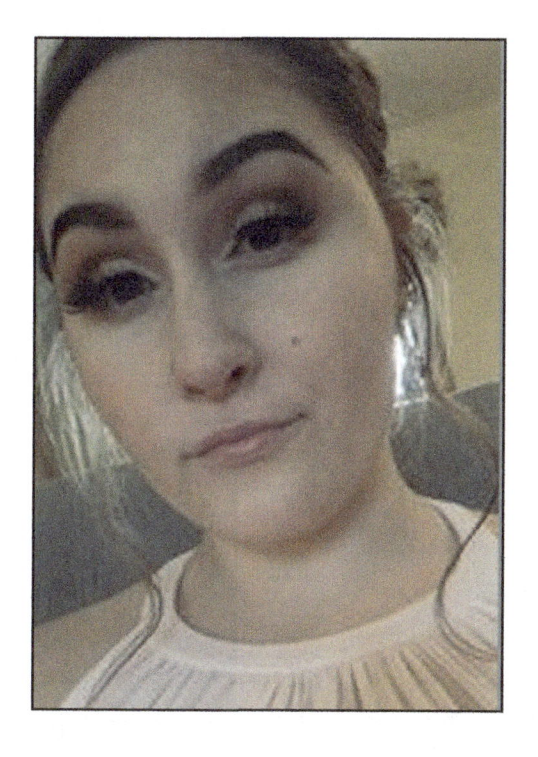

I'm Matthew Gezequel, a police officer for the city of Sandusky, Michigan, and I've been doing that for 25 years.

Our daughter Alexis (Lexi, or "Lex") was the sweetest child I can imagine. She was a little sports fan. Before she was a year old, she was sitting in one of those little bouncy chairs and we were watching a Red Wings hockey game. That was the year they won it all. My wife, Jen, is a huge Red Wings fan. There was the go-ahead goal, and Lexi reacted before we did! She was flailing her little arms, and she was just as excited as she could be.

After Lexi passed, we had an outpouring of people who came to support me, Jen, and the family. Surprisingly, we had so many people who contacted us who just wanted to tell us about Lex. And I found out that apparently, she befriended every foreign exchange student at Central Michigan University. She had friends all over the world. And all of them had the same story, "She was the friend I didn't know I needed." And, "She was the best friend I ever had." We live in a small rural community in the thumb of Michigan, and one of her best friends had to come out of the closet on his own. Nobody else was there to support him. The only one that did was Lexi, who kept telling him, "You be you. It doesn't matter how anybody else thinks. It's how you feel." That was part of Lexi's love.

Lexi passed from this world on November 14, 2021.

We thought Lexi had asthma as a child. Later, when she got to college, she was diagnosed with lupus. Later still, she had blood clots in her lungs due to birth control pills. So, she stopped the birth control and soon after, she became pregnant ... with twins! Twin girls, as we later learned.

On the day she passed, we were five hours away helping her brother move. She was nineteen weeks pregnant. Her fiancé called us and urgently pleaded with us to come home. We asked him what was wrong, but he could hardly speak. Not knowing what to say or how to tell us, he said she broke her leg. Then, he passed the phone to a paramedic, who reported, "She's cold." I'm a police officer, and I understood those words. Right then, I knew the story. We had to make the rest of that five-hour drive knowing Lexi had passed.

We got home and found two police officers waiting at our house. Since it's a small community, I recognized them...I had trained with them years before. They were dumbfounded; they gave us both hugs and we went inside.

An autopsy revealed that Lexi had passed from multiple pulmonary embolisms: blood clots in the lungs.

<< Deep Breath>>

Fast forward a few months. There was a dilapidated butterfly garden that had been created by the Boy Scouts as an Eagle Scout project. It had been about three years since it was built, and I would walk past this thing almost every day thinking, "This could be so much nicer." When Lexi passed, I went

16 Lexi's Dad, Matt G.

to the City Manager and said, "I want that butterfly garden." He looked at me and asked, "What will you do with it?" I answered, "We'll plant new trees and flowers in the garden to attract butterflies."

We went in, three Department of Public Works guys and me, and cleared the path from edge to edge. We brought in three truckloads of soil, then planted, and mulched the entire garden. We brought in many new plants and trees and transplanted the ones that could be repurposed to attract butterflies. We put a ton of work into this little garden area. On Memorial Day–Lexi's 25th birthday–we held a cookout. We asked everyone who was invited to bring a plant for the garden.

That garden is the one place I've been able to heal. I'll go out there some days when I'm off work; if I get off at three in the morning, I go out there and just sit on that bench. Next, I'll realize it's five a.m. because I was so at peace sitting there. We hear the same thing from other people. One person described it as if you can feel the love in that garden. It's just like a peaceful, loving spa treatment–being in that garden…our "fairy garden."

How did we deal with Lexi's passing? Ugh. As I mentioned, I'm a police officer, but because our department is so small, I am also a medical examiner. So, when we got home and saw her, I realized that even if I'd been standing right there with an AED (Automated External Defibrillator), I couldn't have brought her back. And then, I realized that her two little dogs had been there as well, so distressed. I could tell that one of Lexi's dogs had been laying on her. Someone asked, "How do you know that?" I answered, "Because, even after all that time, there was an area right here on her chest that was still warm." The only way that could have happened is if something warm was laying there with her. That would be Teddy, Lexi's little 7-pound Yorkie. He was her best friend.

As far as ways I've tried to heal, I think helping other people is one of the most healing things any of us can do. I got "busy" and signed up to teach a class called Sexual Harassment, Assault, and Rape Prevention. And now, I'm doing a personal defense course. I'm also working out more whether I want to or not. I'm doing more exercising, but I'm also doing things that I realize can help more people. With my experience, I can educate people on how to understand fear. Probably one of the things that helped me most was when I took a class called No Fear, which is spelled KNOW Fear! Everything we do is focused on fear, and understanding your biggest fears gives you a huge advantage in life. Somebody asked me, "Now that you've taken this class, what's your biggest fear? Is it death like everybody else?" I looked at him and replied, "Hell, no. I'm not afraid of death at all. I'm not going to go looking for it, but at the same time, I sure as hell ain't afraid of it." I continued, "My biggest fear is loss. I don't want to lose my son; I don't want to lose my wife." I have no control over either one. But now I can try and help others understand how and what they're dealing with, and then help them realize what their fears might be. This made me a better police officer, for sure. But it's also made me a better human being. Knowing myself at a deeper level has also helped me understand and deal with my grief.

What have I learned from this experience? I have a tattoo on my arm which says "Love, Laugh, Live". This one is from Lexi. She enjoyed every minute of every day. She had the Live, Laugh, Love sign in her room. But she didn't like that sign the way it was made, because she kept saying the order was wrong. She said, "It's Love, Laugh, Live." I asked, "How do you figure that?" Lex answered, "You love first. Because once you love, you're going to laugh. And that's when you live." She explained that doing it in the other order was wrong. Smart!

We heard it said many times that Lexi was an old soul. I've learned to try and be more like her, and I think that's helped me, both as a police officer and as a human being. It's helped me as a father and as a husband.

A little story about signs. We had a picture taken in the garden. Later, when we looked at it carefully, you can literally see a set of wings, a pink set of wings in the clouds above the garden. And then, in the middle of the picture, there's an orb. People explained it away by saying there was something on the camera lens. But neither the prior picture nor the subsequent photos had the same image. So, that seems to make the "something on the lens" story

16 Lexi's Dad, Matt G.

impossible.

We've had a couple of readings with psychic mediums where Lexi's come through to us. In one of those readings, the medium talked about "the two little ones." I understood this to be the unborn twin girls, whom we named Chevelle and Riviera. Then, about a week after that reading, I was in bed, and at around 1:30 in the morning I had this weird feeling, so I opened my eyes. Background: When Lexi was little, she was famous for coming into our room, standing as close to you as possible, and just staring at you. She wouldn't touch you, but you'd wake up with that weird feeling, knowing somebody was staring at you. Well, I woke up at this particular time, and I looked up to see this little girl staring at me. It was Lexi's face, but she had curly jet-black hair. The only way she could curl it is if she paid for a perm or if somebody put curlers in her hair. Lexi's hair was black, but perfectly straight, just like her mother's. To see this vision of a face with these perfect curls and ringlets around her face...it woke me up out of a dead sleep. I sat up and I was trying to reach for her. Then it was gone. I sat there, and I'm like, "OK, let's go back to sleep. Let's continue this dream." I went back to sleep and had this dream that Jen and I were at the Detroit Zoo. That's something we always did with Lexi and her brother, Christian. In the dream, I hear this little voice that says, "Oh, look at the Tangaroa." (Neither Lexi nor Christian could say the word "kangaroo" properly at that young age). There they were in my dream, talking about this Tangaroa. So, I look over and again, I see this curly-haired child with Lexi's face. Standing next to her is another little girl with red hair. The redheaded child looked just like my wife when she was little, with freckles and everything. I mean, it was like an identical image of my wife, but with reddish hair. Lexi would always joke that if she ever had girls, she hoped one would have curly hair. And she always said 'I'm going to have a redheaded one'.

We believe this little girl was Lexi's way of portraying one of the twins. We always represent Chevelle as a monarch butterfly, and we represent Riviera as a yellow tiger swallowtail. And that's how they're represented on Lexi's headstone as well. We paid tribute to all three of them by including the butterflies on Lexi's headstone.

One time when I was working the night shift, there was a call for a runaway child just outside the city limits. This was about 7:00 p.m., and no one took the call; everybody was tied up. Finally, they turned to me at 9:00 p.m. and asked, "Hey, can you go check on this kid?" So, I contacted the mother and she admitted, "He was really pissed off at me, we're pretty sure he just walked." The family had been at that address only six months. Three weeks after they moved in, the kid's father passed away. He was just 13 years old. Half a mile away there was a stand of woods behind the mom's house. So, we had three fire trucks and two sheriff's deputies show up to help search those woods. Fire truck lights! Police lights! We were there for three hours. We found nothing and decided to wait and see if the kid would simply come home. At 1:30 in the morning, that's what happened. The mother called to inform me, but she also wanted me to talk to her son. I agreed to go over to the house.

While we were talking, I asked him, "Did you know we were out looking for you?" He said "Yeah, I kind of figured. I saw all the fire trucks, and people going in and out of the woods. I was sitting out in the middle of this ..."

I interrupted him: "The butterfly garden?"

He said, "Yeah, that garden. Right in the middle. I was sitting on the bench. I was able to just sit and feel. My anger at my mom kind of went away. I could feel my dad talking to me and telling me, "You know, you've got to be a big brother. You can't act like this."

"So, you were sitting on the bench in the middle of the butterfly garden?" I asked.

He replied, "Yep. Do you know the butterfly garden?"

I smiled and said, "Oh, yeah, I know it. As a matter of fact, the bench you were sitting on is in memory of my daughter, Alexis, and her twin daughters, Chevelle and Riviera."

He started crying and I nearly started crying at the same time, and he just hugged me. Then, his mom came over and gave us both a hug.

I explained to him, "I don't normally say stuff like this, but if you ever need to talk to somebody, I want you to understand, I will sit down and talk

16 Lexi's Dad, Matt G.

with you."

We talked about the spat he had had with his mom. She had taken his phone because he had broken the rules. He pouted and ran away. He regretted it. "I need to act like the big brother and be a good example for my sister from now on."

I've talked to him a couple times since. The last time I talked with him, I was out working in that garden. He was walking through it, and he told me he was bringing his little sister with him to show her the fairy garden (that's another name we have for it). You know, I've done so many things in my career and in my life that I'm proud of. To have that guy, that little guy, say those things, and still be willing to talk to me has meant more than anything else. That garden doesn't just heal me and my wife and my family. It's helping to heal a community!

I keep telling my wife, Jen, the same thing over and over. I have more to offer! Being a part of the Helping Fathers Heal group has helped me greatly. I lost my dad in 2005. I lost my mom in 2012. My dad was my rock. Still, to this day, I will talk to my father. And I know he talks back. From the medium readings and things that we've read, the one thing that we've heard from everybody is that Lexi is never alone in her spirit world. My dad and my mom are right there with her.

Some days you just want to sit there and scream. And you can't. In my job, there are days you just can't. You can't break down and cry. But afterward, you sit there and you're just numb. You know, it's nice to have this group (Helping Fathers Heal). I can tell you, I've recommended this to probably 10 or 15 people that I know. I tell them that when they're ready, this is where I strongly suggest they go.

Lexi's brother, Christian, had another very interesting sign. He plays these role-playing video games. He's got a monitor that displays 3D images on the screen. I'd like to close by sharing the following story in his words.

"I'm playing the video game and I get an error code in my headset. I look at the screen and it's showing me an image of somebody else sitting in my chair. Lexi? Then, the image goes away. A little later, there's another error on the screen. And

again, there's somebody sitting in my chair. Suddenly, two little figures popped up next to my legs, and my legs went ice cold. They're small...they're only coming up to my knee. Then, they're grabbing my legs, and I can feel it. I sat down in the chair; it was ice cold. I was just sitting there, and Lexi gave me a whack across the back of the head. And I said, 'That's enough!'"

17 Matthew's Dad, Dan D.

    Matthew is the oldest of my two boys, and honestly, I haven't decided how I'm going to reconcile the age equation when my youngest son surpasses him in living years. As I sit here writing these words today, it's been nearly 17 months since my son passed due to a fentanyl overdose on Father's Day.

    Matthew's story began long before he was born. It began before Lisa and I were married. It began even before we started dating if you can imagine that. Matthew's tale began back in 1992 when my wife, who was a friend and incidentally my neighbor at the time, was assigned a project for her high school Home Economics class to care for a make-believe newborn baby constructed out of a bag of flour wearing a onesie. Lisa asked me if I would volunteer to share parenting responsibilities with her and I agreed. We named our flour baby Matthew, and I guess we never looked back. From then on, he was simply destined to be.

Our real-life Matthew was born in November of 1999 with all the wonderment, joy, hopes, and dreams that two new parents in their early 20s could possibly have had. He was the apple of my eye. He is, was, and will forever be, my everything.

Our son became the center of our world, and there he would remain until the day he passed. As a small child, he had our undivided attention for five years before his brother, Randy, was born. This means we doted over him like crazy and admittedly spoiled him to the best of our ability. Albeit a rambunctious, high-energy, mischievous, little-rascal-kind-of-kid, he had a happy childhood where he was loved deeply and unconditionally by both his parents, his dog Sonny, and his extended family. Despite the joy he was to our lives, it wasn't lost on my wife and me that he was a born rebel and a consummate rule-breaker.

I'm glossing over the fact that Matthew was a difficult baby, toddler, small child, adolescent, and young adult. Add to that, we were young parents operating without a handbook. We made mistakes along the way. Matthew made mistakes as well. It arguably might have been a contest for him to see who would make the most mistakes.

From a very young age, it was clear that Matthew didn't really understand rules, and if he did, he certainly didn't intend to follow them; and even if he did follow them, it would be on his terms. Later in life, this would actually be diagnosed as an Oppositional Defiant Disorder (ODD).

Matthew was shockingly smart, and when you combine that with a splash of defiance, you're going to get some interesting outcomes. But that didn't mean it wasn't without entertainment, at least in retrospect. One time in daycare, the subject matter was potty training, and all the kids were supposed to use the restroom (I picture a potty line). I think they called it the potty train. Matthew turned and purposely peed on a kid who was making fun of him. This might have been our actual first time being called into the

17 Matthew's Dad, Dan D.

principal's office, but there would be more, a lot more. Matthew once hid a walkie-talkie under his younger brother's bed to scare him. When we calmed his brother down and checked under his bed, we missed it, twice, and kept sending him back to bed. After that, we had an unspoken rule in our house, "Don't pull pranks on Matthew!" It was understood that, in a contest, his opponent was going to lose and there was no telling where it would lead and whether the authorities were going to be involved.

When he was six years old, I gifted him an old computer when I upgraded my own. I remember thinking, how can that be a bad thing? I loaded a few age-appropriate games, Mickey Mouse playhouse kind of stuff, and he learned the basics while other kids his age were probably stacking wooden blocks. This would lead to at least one memorable story. When Matthew was just eight, he applied for a credit card and came perilously close to getting one. His plan was only foiled by a social security number and an annual income value that were missing a few digits–something my wife found out about when the company called to confirm the missing numbers.

All in all, throughout Matthew's early adolescence, our family was living a dream, although, at the time, we didn't know it. We took vacations and made meaningful and positive memories that will last us a lifetime. At the same time, though, Matthew also presented us with mounting behavioral problems stemming from his ODD.

Matthew's teenage years were tough on us. He began experimenting with drugs at just 14, probably to self-medicate from anxiety and depression borne out of low self-esteem and bullying. The world is cruel. People are cruel. Kids are cruel. Matthew was born with a birthmark on his left cheek. He endured teasing for most of his younger years, some of which he surely brought upon himself, some because of the way he looked. He was skinny, he didn't dress like other kids, he had braces, he had glasses, he had big ears, etc. He could move his ears, by the way. Seriously, those things were big, and he could really get them flapping.

In any case, Matthew became very self-conscious, and I suspect those thoughts played a part in the choices he made that would put him on a path toward drugs and addiction.

My son passed away in June of 2022 at the age of 22 following his longest stretch of sobriety in his adult life. Unfortunately, it was his seemingly successful rehabilitation that same year that allowed my wife and I to lower our guard to the point that we foolishly felt he was safe. I will always carry an insurmountable amount of guilt surrounding the details of my son's passing. I am plagued by blame and shame that I attach to myself that, now, just 17 months later, doesn't seem likely to subside to any measurable degree. I was there for my son when he needed me for every day of his 22 years, except for the one day he needed me most, and for whatever moment of weakness he had that led him to relapse. I have profound regret, and although I'm ready to move toward healing, I'm not yet in a place where much works. Matthew passed alone, seemingly comfortable, on a bed wearing pajamas I had seen him wear a million times before, his cell phone nearby, maybe listening to music. I won't ever know exactly.

Following my son's passing, I think I must have been in a state of shock. I don't know how we got through planning the funeral, attending the funeral, speaking at the funeral, and ultimately coming home to a house he would never physically be in again, in a world where I would never be able to hold him again. The first few months were a blur. I tried to go back to work a few weeks later only to come to the realization that I was in no shape to do so. I later took an extended leave of absence where I pursued grief counseling and sought the help of a psychiatrist.

Seventeen months later I'm uncertain if I am better, worse, or the same, but I have been told not to think about myself in those terms. Grief counseling led me to investigate and join an organization called GRASP (Grief Recovery After a Substance Passing), and GRASP led me to investigate and join an organization called Helping Fathers Heal, which is how I find myself here today writing these words. I've learned there's no magic bullet for grief, but I have found solace in the shared stories of both organizations. There's value in knowing you're not alone in these circumstances. For me, I know it's a place where I can be honest about how I am feeling at any given moment, even if

17 Matthew's Dad, Dan D.

that particular moment is a pity party. You see, the rest of the world doesn't know this kind of anguish unless they've experienced this kind of anguish. This translates to a lack of understanding they cannot make up for, even the ones who are wanting and willing to try.

When I think about advice for someone who is having to live through this experience, my first thought is that I'm no expert, not feeling very successful in my own story, but I would say you have to do something, versus nothing. My personal goal was to try everything on the off chance that I'd get a little bit of a positive takeaway from all efforts combined. I knew that if I didn't take a proactive approach, I had almost no hope of moving forward. So, there you have it, my advice is to try everything that stands a chance of having a positive impact. Some things will work better than others, but don't give up on the pursuit.

When it comes to signs, I'm a skeptic. I genuinely want to believe in them. When I tell you what I've experienced, you might think I'm actually pretty dense to consider dismissing some of these as coincidences. But I cannot help my nature, which is to question, versus accept. So here goes...

First, some context:

1) Matthew is tech-savvy and,

2) Many of the lights in my house employ smart switches that can be turned on/off with verbal commands shouted to Alexa devices.

In the days following Matthew's passing, I found out that when these smart plug devices lose internet connectivity they blink bright blue until they reconnect. So that's exactly what happened multiple times per night between 3 a.m. and 4 a.m. for approximately 30 consecutive days. Between the Alexa devices and the smart plugs blinking, my room lit up as if it were a disco for 20-30 seconds at a time each night. As noted, this went on for about a month, and while it interrupted my sleep for sure, it was comforting to feel that Matthew was communicating with me the best he could. It still happens to this day, but now it only seems to coincide with me asking him to let me know he's OK, or when I'm particularly upset. There've been other things here and there, but this one gets me every time.

On the topic of medium readings, I believe I have been able to directly communicate with my son, but I'm also firmly of the belief that not everyone who claims to be a medium is indeed legitimate. My experience having met with a few is that they can range from amazing to mediocre to predatory, and as such, your best bet is to go with one that is referred and recommended by multiple independent sources. When you meet with the right person it can be an enlightening, emotional experience hearing someone you just met tell you things that only you and your child would know as if the words were coming directly from him to you.

As I close this passage dedicated to my son Matthew, I do so with deep gratitude to the gentlemen who are there for me from Helping Fathers Heal. Though I may not attend every meeting, it's comforting to know they are only a text message or phone call away.

18 Mike's Dad, Steven L.

Mike was a very funny kid growing up. He was always having fun with us and with his friends. He was not the most outgoing kid around, but once he got comfortable, he would always enjoy himself. He liked to play video games and got very good at doing the dances in the game, "Fortnite." We used to laugh so much at those dances. His friends said he was great, and better than them at it, too.

Our relationship was awesome. I liked to think of both my children as not just my kids, but my best friends, too.

Mike and I loved to go dirt bike riding together. We got a Honda 70cc for Christmas, and we would ride together out in the woods.

Another thing he loved to do with me was to go shooting. I taught both my kids proper firearm safety at an early age, and all of us would go either to the range or into the woods to shoot. After a while, my daughter, Nicole, wanted to do her own thing and so it became just Mike and me. My boy was a great shot!

Mike transitioned on Friday, May 18, 2018, by his own hand. He was just home from camp and seemed fine. He never showed any signs of mental illness. He got mad at his video game, and I had to take away his game controllers. We argued, said things we wished we hadn't, and I left to go to the store. While I was gone, Mike got a rope from his suitcase and hanged himself from his loft bed. Nicole discovered him. He was already gone. The paramedics tried to save him, but they couldn't. Mike was only eleven years old when he left us.

I remember the morning after he passed. I looked out the window at the world continuing to carry on…it was unreal, like I was watching a TV program. I felt like a balloon that had just been popped. None of the people I was watching had any idea of what had just happened. For them, it was only another day of running around, going to work, shopping, taking the kids out, or going to Grandma's. It was like I was dreaming–a nightmare, really. The task of calling all his friends' parents fell upon me. It was one of the hardest things I've ever had to do.

The first three months were a blur. I was living in a fog. One hundred percent in denial. I thought I would wake up one day and discover that it was all a dream and that he was alive and well. I felt like a part of me had been cut away, and I wasn't a complete person anymore. Each day just going through the motions. Crying at the drop of a hat. Everything was a trigger. Going to the store and seeing things I would normally buy for him and beginning to reach for them, only to remember he wasn't here anymore. I still bought those things for a while. I guess it was part of the denial. "If I buy things for him, maybe he will come back." At that point, I felt completely lost. Every minute was a reminder that Mike was gone.

My family was very supportive. They still are, but you will find that people slowly start to go back to their routines. They visit less and call infrequently, until the day when they stop altogether. Not because they don't care. For them, the tragedy is just not as close. They still have lives and responsibilities of their own. They don't live the loss every day like we do. I also think that they're afraid bringing it up will cause us pain. The truth is, we are always in pain, and it's worse when it seems that everyone else is forgetting about our child. The very thing they don't do (because they think it will hurt us) is what ends up hurting us the most.

I've noticed that other parents often seem to fade away faster than those without children. I think it's because we scare them. A parent's worst fear is losing a child. And when it happens to someone they know, it is a stark reminder that it can happen to any parent, no matter how good or attentive you are. For that reason, they run from us.

People say dumb things and I'm sure they mean well. "Well, you just have to let them go." How exactly am I supposed to do that? "It's time for you to move on." Move on to what? "I lost my grandmother last year, so I know exactly how you feel." Really? What aspirations did you have for your grandmother's life, I wonder? Were you looking forward to seeing her grow up and start a family or go to college?

The worst one for me is, "I lost my pet recently, so I know what you are going through." I love my pets just as much as anyone else, but it's not a comparison by any means. I had to make the conscious choice to understand that these people have the best intentions with their asinine comments or suggestions. They just don't understand, and they don't know what to say, so they revert to things you might say to someone in other situations where a loved one has passed. The problem is that none of them give comfort. It's different when it's your own child.

Over time, we get better at handling the waves of emotions. It's like going to the gym. As you lift a heavy weight over and over, it gets easier to manage with time. But the fact is, the weight still weighs the same. It didn't get lighter, you got stronger.

I had support from my family and friends, but there is really very little they can do. There is nothing they can say. Just being with us is the most healing. Maybe an act of kindness, like taking some of the daily responsibilities away from us for a while (like cooking, etc.). Eventually, they go back to their own lives.

I felt totally lost. I was the one that had to be strong for my wife, Daisy, and our daughter. I was not able to process my grief for a long time. I was more concerned for them. I also blamed myself for what happened, so I felt I didn't deserve "the luxury" of grieving. It took a long time for that to fade, but I don't think I will ever completely stop feeling that way.

I never sought counseling, although Daisy did for a while. I know that many people have had great experiences with grief counselors, but for us, it was not helpful. It really depends on the counselor.

Finding Helping Parents Heal (HPH) and then getting involved with Helping Fathers Heal (HFH) have been the best resources for me. I like being part of a group of men who all wish they'd met under different circumstances but still come together to support each other. It's an unbreakable brotherhood. I try to get to the weekly meeting online and, whether or not I interact, I always come away with something that helps me keep going. I am blessed to be a part of it.

I've learned that I can survive anything. I have been through much in my life, but nothing compares to the loss of a child. I have learned that I am more resilient than I thought. I have learned that my relationship with God is stronger than I imagined. I have learned that my family can come together again. I have learned that I can still help other people even when I am a molten lump of goo inside. It's been quite a journey just getting past the five-year mark.

After some time, I learned that I could sort of be like my old self. It is hard to regain the life you had before the loss. After Mike passed, I was sure I would never laugh again. Then one day, I heard a news story about a truck that overturned on the highway, spilling 20 tons of chicken feathers on the road, creating havoc for morning traffic. The video made me laugh. When I realized I had laughed, I knew there was hope.

The thing that has most surprised me is how differently each person deals with the loss. It's hard to hash out in words, but it is one of the things that grieving parents understand. I was able to console myself and not blame

God. I've had a lot of practice doing those things. I learned that many other people I know also had children who had passed. We exchanged stories, and I learned their perspectives and their processes for living beyond the loss.

As far as advice for other Dads, I would begin by saying, "Just breathe." Take it slow. There is no rush to do anything other than what is needed when someone we love leaves us. You will be at this for the rest of your life. Just gather yourself and be the man you need to be for those around you. Most families turn to the father figure for support and strength, and now is the time to be there for them. In the first few weeks, there are so many things to do, and no one will have the strength to do them. Funeral planning. The actual funeral. Placing them where you want them, whether it's in a cemetery or at home. How to deal with their belongings. How to tell their friends, and maybe even friends' families. Do what you can. Be there as you can. Just do what is needed in the now, because time will work out the details. Yet be aware of yourself, too. As men, we may want to close down. Sometimes that's for the best, but sometimes it's not healthy. At some point, you'll start to better understand yourself, and what you are going through as you deal with such a loss in your life. Just take it slow. Breathe. Time marches on whether we want it to or not. It's hard to believe, but you WILL survive this. Trust that your child is there with you. They say time heals all wounds. Well, Time, let's see what you can do with this one! I'm finding out, day by day.

I have found a lot of healing power in getting back to the things Mike and I used to enjoy together. That is probably one of the hardest things to do, though. We may not want to do anything that we used to enjoy with our child, because they are not here with us. But the thing is, they ARE HERE! It takes a while, but when you start to do those things again you will find that they are some of the most therapeutic things you can do for yourself, and for your connection to your child on the other side. There is a serious emotional learning curve, though.

Another helpful thing for me was keeping up the relationships that were important to Mike. We used to have parties at our house for all the birthdays, holidays, and celebrations. Mike's friends' families would all come over. We kept those going for several years. I also continue to be a part of my son's best friend's life. His name is Kelven, and we've known him since he was in preschool. We help each other stay connected to Mike and we have a lot of fun when we get to hang out for a while. These relationships are important. Try not to let them fade.

We have received some incredible signs from Mike. The chicken feather story I told you about connected me to him when I later remembered Mike's nickname in gaming, Mr. Chixens! He thought it sounded funnier than Mr. Chickens. There were other chicken signs, like pictures of campfire flames that took on the shape of a chicken.

The first major sign was during a prayer ceremony. Daisy is Filipino and a practicing Catholic, and they have a ritual that includes ten days of prayer. We would burn a candle every day, and a group of people came to our home each day to read a prayer. On the tenth day, as I was getting ready for bed, I went to put the candle out. I saw that it had burned down on the inside and somehow, a portion of the candle and the wick fell out the bottom, still lit! A shaman told me that it meant that Mike's light had gone out early, but it was still burning on the other side. That is strange, but no one saw it happen, or how it happened. But this wasn't the only candle sign from Mike.

At the one-year "Angelversary" date, Filipino tradition called for us to do the prayer ceremony again. On the tenth day, as we sat praying, the candle was burning near the bottom and then turned into a long "blow torch" type of flame with a point of blue light - like a star - at the top of that flame. Then it went out. I have never seen that happen before! Even the leader, who had been leading prayer ceremonies for over 30 years, had never seen anything like it. I asked my shaman friend about it, and he explained that Mike is "complete as a Spirit." It was incredible.

One day at the cemetery I discovered a coffee mug on Mike's headstone. The mug graphics displayed "You're the best dad." That was what we would say to each other every day when I dropped Mike off at school. I would tell him, "You're the best son!" And he would say back, "You're the best dad!" We asked everyone we knew who could have put that mug there. No one had a clue.

Indulge me in one more story about incredible signs. Daisy and I had been visiting Mike's grave daily and each time, we placed a rock on his headstone. With each new visit, we noticed that the rock we had previously placed now had bird droppings on it. Only on that one stone. Birds were doing target practice! During one visit, we were standing near Mike's grave when I looked up at the sky and saw a cloud shaped exactly like a heart. I pointed it out to Daisy and joked, "Is that cloud full of bird crap?" A few minutes later, she said, "Come here. You have to see this." I went over to find on his newest stone one single splat of bird poop, and it was in the shape of an "M". We couldn't believe it, but there it was, plain as day. When you think about the chances of a splat of bird crap looking like anything, much less a letter in the alphabet, the one letter that his name started with, oriented in the correct alignment so it could be read; it was just unbelievable. I have shown the picture to hardened skeptics, and even they say they can't explain that one. A medium later told us that Mike has a connection with birds. We told her this story and she laughed, "Mike's telling you that you don't have to go there to be with him."

I've also had visions of Mike visiting us since he's passed. We've had experiences of weird shadows in the house, but this time was different. I was going down the hall to wake our daughter and as I passed by Mike's room, I glanced in and saw him standing by his bed with his back to me. He was leaning over as if he was picking something up. I saw it clear as day. I stopped and looked more closely, but then there was no one there. I felt a cold chill and said, "I saw you, Mike!"

In our interactions with mediums, we've been able to get an answer to the question many of us ask ourselves. Why did he do it? What we've heard was this–he did not really intend to take his life. Mike was just acting out. He was only eleven, after all. He didn't understand that what he was about to do was going to end his life. It was a terrible mistake.

Many people believe we each have a "soul plan" when we come into this life. We decide how it will go, what we will learn, who our family and teachers will be, and most importantly, when we will leave. So, if you go along with this idea, then Mike chose from the get-go not to be here on the earth for a long life. Even harder to understand is that our whole family agreed to experience this together before we arrived here on the earth. As we talked about all the things we wished we had done to stop it, a medium explained something valuable to us—even if we had intervened, Mike would have left another way shortly thereafter. It was his choice before he was even born. After thinking about this, we realized there were a lot of indicators that this could be true.

This world and "the other side" are still mysteries to me. However, I know now without a single doubt that the other side exists. I also know that Mike is with all the other family members who have passed. Someday, I will be with Mike again. I am in no hurry, but I have no fear at all now. And I can't wait to see him.

19 Tyler's Dad, Will T.

My son, Tyler, was the kind of person who cared and loved deeply. He would give you the shirt off his back. I had a great relationship with him. We talked about all manner of things: obscure videos he found on YouTube, anime, war history. There was no conversation I couldn't have with Tyler.

My favorite memory of Tyler was when I met him for the first time. We met while I was dating his mom, Lisa. She first introduced us when he was two years old. He just watched me for a while. Then, out of nowhere, he came over and put his arm on my shoulder, and said, "What's up?" We have been close since that day.

Tyler had an extraordinary amount of energy growing up. But sometimes that energy was over the top. He would run around our apartment at full speed and then use the walls to stop. Lisa and I would ask him, "Why would you do that?" He joked, "So I can stop."

As a child, like many kids, he loved Pokemon. That led to Dragonball Z and eventually to a keen interest in anime.

Tyler loved sports, and he always yearned to be outside. He also loved–and I mean LOVED–chocolate. He could smell chocolate, even wrapped chocolate. He would come home from school, take a sniff, and say, "There's chocolate in the house." Lisa and I would ask him, "How do you know that?" And Tyler would answer, "I just know." And then he would look for it, invariably finding it. Once, he even found a chocolate bar that was in the freezer!

Tyler moved out when he was 26. At his new place, there was a confrontation with a roommate that escalated, and the roommate was hurt. Tyler was arrested and had to wear an ankle monitor.

Tyler was physically, emotionally, and mentally abused by his girlfriend, who claimed she loved him even more than we did. Lisa and I believe that she was the one who introduced him to illicit narcotics.

On the day of his transition, that very morning, Lisa had a massive panic attack. We couldn't figure out why. Later that day, before I left to go to work, Tyler's ankle monitor beeped because it needed to be charged. It had never beeped before, so we went into his room to see what was going on and found him on the bed. Lisa knew right away that he was gone and screamed, "Call 911!"

Two days later, the girlfriend showed up at our house demanding to know where Tyler was and why he hadn't called her. That's when Lisa confronted her. First, she tried to deny it. Then, she confessed to us that she gave him fentanyl and he didn't know. We think she put it in his drink and that's how this all happened.

The first months after Tyler transitioned were pure agony. I couldn't imagine how we would be able to move, let alone continue to live our lives

19 Tyler's Dad, Will T.

without our son. Tyler was a brother to Kayla, Ariana, and Trysten, and he was an uncle to Kaydence and Kassidy. My wife was inconsolable, and my first thought was to be the strong one. But in doing so, it made me seem like his death wasn't affecting me as much as everyone else. My wife told me how our girls thought I didn't care, and it broke my heart. So, I started to show more emotion. We went through the different stages of grief, sometimes two or three times. For quite a while, Lisa would fantasize, telling me to "go get him and apologize for her" and "tell him to just come home." She would beg me to tell her "This is not real", but I couldn't do that. I told her it wouldn't be fair to her if I lied and told her something that wasn't true.

In the beginning, everyone was trying to be supportive, but then people slowly stopped calling and checking on us. When we would ask why, they would reply that they didn't know what to say. We would let them know that there was nothing they could say to help us feel better, but just letting us know they were there was enough. I'm not going to lie, I thought that because my family is so large and had seen its share of death, we would've gotten more support. My wife's family is much smaller and younger than mine, so her family hasn't suffered as much death and grief. Surprisingly, we have been getting more support from other parents who are in the same situation.

I've learned that grieving is different for everyone. I have lost my grandparents, my mother, and my brother. Although it hurt to lose them, the pain does not compare to the loss of my son. I also realized I have to show more emotion than I'm used to with my wife and other children. It's not that I don't show any emotion. It probably has to do with my attitude about "being the man of the house." To me, that meant showing some emotion, but not letting it all out because of some male ideology of what strength is supposed to look like. *Stay in control!*

The most surprising thing is the number of bonds we have formed with other grieving parents. Those have been a real comfort. My wife and I have made new friends and have helped them, as they have helped us, through this never-ending process. My family and friends have not shown the level of interest in how our lives have been since our son's transition. I do understand they may not know what to say and what not to say. Here's the thing, nothing is being said at all. I would rather get a call saying "Hi," or a text asking, "How are you?" That is not happening. We have asked family and friends to do those things just so we'll know that they are there for us.

As far as advice for other fathers going through the same thing, I would say it's okay to let your feelings out. Don't feel like you have to be the strong, silent man of the house. I did that and it wasn't the right thing to do. You have to let your emotions out because if you don't, it may end up hurting you or someone you love. If you have other children, don't forget they lost a sibling, too. And although your pain is that of a parent, understand that theirs is different but not less than yours. It will take time for everyone to get to a place where they can get through the day, but that happens at a different pace for everyone.

When it comes to practices that have helped me heal, just a couple of thoughts. Remember what I said about being "the man"? Well, sometimes that is needed. It helps me to find relief and healing when I can be there for my wife when she's having a rough day. She confides her feelings whether good, bad, or indifferent, and it makes me feel good to let her know her feelings are safe with me. I would never make her think her feelings are wrong or invalid.

We're amazed that Tyler has sent us so many signs. There's the light in the china cabinet that turns on by itself. The TV in his room was on the other day, and the remotes were all in the holder. My wife saw his reflection on her iPad screen, and she said it felt like he hugged her because she felt a chill and got goosebumps, but the chill came from the inside, not like when you normally get goosebumps.

There are moments when I can hear his voice. For instance, we used to talk in the morning, not about anything in particular. But sometimes, I hear him saying things to me from the spot where he always liked to stand, right behind the couch in the family room. Just before he passed, he shared a song with Lisa. That song was deep and cerebral, and it described how he felt about her. In the lyrics, Tyler apologized to her for not knowing how to say how he felt. Also, when I hear certain songs that I like, I can hear him saying, "That

19 Tyler's Dad, Will T.

song is stupid." Or when I'm looking for something to watch on TV, I will scroll through anime because he loved it, and I would see one and feel him nudging me to watch it. I do... and I enjoy it.

I would also like to acknowledge all the grieving fathers in the Helping Fathers Heal Group for their continued support while going through this difficult time for us all. It's really helped me. I miss my Tyler.

20 Noah's Dad, Bunt T.

My son Noah is a kind and gentle soul. He was at times a leader and at other times a homebody who didn't want to go out and interact. He always put others before himself. Noah was the kind of kid who would open doors for people without ever being told. He just came into this world with a sense of manners and maturity. He was kind and polite to most everyone. His level of respect for others was way beyond his years. I think of him as an old soul. It surprised me that a pre-teen young boy would be into jazz music instead of the popular stuff on the radio. He would crank up Kenny G and relax with his video games. I'd ask him, "What are you listening to?" He would just shrug and smile. He was a good kid in so many ways, and I really miss him.

Noah's beautiful face is very expressive. I used to laugh out loud at his goofy expressions, and he still makes them; I see them. When I do something dumb, he gets after me, and I know he's laughing at me.

Noah passed away on February 11, 2023, at the age of 13. As of this writing, it's only been nine months that I've been adjusting to this new life without my son. He was undergoing treatments since being diagnosed with acute lymphoblastic leukemia (A.L.L.) in 2022. When he passed, he only had one treatment left. I also have two older children who primarily live on their own or with their mom. They were close to Noah, as well. Having siblings is another layer of complexity in the grieving process.

For the first month after he transitioned, I was lost and heartbroken. I had lost faith in myself…and felt that I had failed as a father. We are supposed to protect our kids. I asked God, "What had I done to be punished like this!" Of all the kids in the world, why did He take my little boy? Of all the bad kids and criminals in the world, why take mine? It reminds me of the song "Only The Good Die Young." But it hurts. This is hard.

How did I go about finding support? Noah's mom and I need to find a better support system. At first, we went to see a grief counselor, but she knew nothing about grieving; she hadn't lost a child. She had no clue about what I was going through. I researched and found my own grief support when I discovered Helping Parents Heal (HPH). HPH then led me to the Helping Fathers Heal Facebook group. In this community, I found a safe zone with all the other dads going through the same thing I am. I finally felt like I was talking with people who understood how I felt. The grief counselors just didn't have that experience.

I also found some peace by having readings with several evidential mediums. I was amazed at some of the things that would come up in those meetings. I think I've connected with Noah in some form every single time. In one of our readings, Noah came through and told us (through the medium) that he was proud of us for putting together the blood drives. We were blown away! This isn't something that a person would know outside of our town. By the way, these blood drives are small local events to honor Noah. During his treatments, blood was in short supply. He needed the blood to help his body recover, but often he would have to wait for an ample supply. So now, by doing these blood drives, it makes me feel good knowing that I'm helping some other kid who may be in Noah's situation. We've done several drives, and so far we average 60-75 pints each time, which is fantastic. Since this honors Noah, it's like therapy for me. We've had people who come and try to give blood, but for one reason or another, they can't donate that day. They come up to me crying and saying, "I'm so sorry, I couldn't do it today." I assure them, "You did what you could. You came because you care and that's all that matters." Thinking about it now gives me the chills. But that IS all that matters to me…just that people cared enough to show up and try to donate blood.

During another medium reading, Noah confirmed that his mom and I were at the hospital with him when he passed. He said, "You were holding me" and then he reassured me that he's okay now, that he's with Grandma, "She helped me over when I passed."

Since it's only been nine months, I often wonder if I'm really doing the grieving work. Should I try to keep myself busy at work and distract myself from the grief? I'm a manager in a local restaurant and my role requires me to mentor the staff, whom I consider to be my "other" kids. This makes me feel good like I can be a sort of father to them. I coach them and ensure that they know what's critical in their jobs in the restaurant. And they appreciate it. I don't think they understand how much I appreciate them. It helps me use that same parental instinct that I used to use with Noah. They're helping me as I grieve.

I've learned a few things along this difficult road, but I'm still new at this and just trying to find peace. This is a hard process that no person should go through alone. You will go through dark times and good times.

What advice would I give other dads? Get help, either with counseling or finding a support system of some kind. I highly recommend connecting with a group that is in the same boat that you are in right now. A group that understands what we are all going through and then keep busy. At least, that's what has kept me sane these past months. I would recommend that you just "go with it" and don't hold back your emotions. You may cry, and there's nothing wrong with that. Let it out. It helps. You don't have to be "strong" all the time. And if you can't cry, don't worry about it. Just try to relax and feel whatever you're feeling. Find some way to find your inner peace.

I try to find peace where and when I can. Usually, my happy, peaceful place is when I visit Noah at the cemetery, which I do several times a week. Sometimes I go every day. I just sit and talk to him…and it brings me closer to him. I feel like he's all around me. I let the world stop for a few minutes and just think about him. And smile. Or cry. Or both.

What helps me most is talking to my son every day. I know he's not physically here, but he is here with me in spirit, and in my mind, and in my heart. I seem to have some "surface-level" medium abilities, and I am trying to develop them. I am working on mediumship skills to be able to get through to Noah. I just want to know that he's not alone in heaven, that he is OK, and that he is well taken care of.

Sometimes when I get quiet and meditate, I just "feel" something coming through from Noah. It may be a phrase or something simple. I once asked a medium if this was, in fact, Noah trying to communicate directly to me, and she said "yes" and that I should continue to develop this listening ability by meditating on Noah and listening for him. I ask him to come and sometimes he does, but it's very subtle. I'm still new at all this.

Outside of work, do things that honor your child. Keep your child alive and top of mind. As I mentioned, I organize and run blood drives to honor Noah. Noah's mom is very artistic and paints colorful rocks. She usually paints images about things that Noah liked, like Mario, SpongeBob SquarePants, Marvel superheroes, and other cartoon characters. Sometimes it's just pretty flowers or butterflies. I lacquer them and put glitter on them. Then we send them all around the world so that others can learn about Noah and follow his Facebook page, #LoveLikeNoah. It helps keep me going. It's another way of honoring Noah.

I believe in signs. Noah and I always have jokes, and certain numbers, like 69, which was one of our inside jokes. He'll send his mom a license that

20 Noah's Dad, Bunt T.

has a 69 and she'll tell me about it, but then for me, he'll make me think about it. I have to work for it. For example, I'll see 3372 (3+3 =6 and 7 + 2 = 9...or "69").

At times when I miss Noah, I ask for more signs, and he will give them to me without me trying to find them. He brings us so many signs: butterflies that just hover in front of my face for what seems like an eternity; or cardinals looking in the windows at me. One day, I was at the cemetery, feeling very upset, and a butterfly flew close to my face for several minutes.

And then there are the squirrels! Noah used to see a squirrel and make a funny comment, using his silly voice to cry "SQUIRREL!" Now, we see them running around at the cemetery and it feels like he's joking around with us. Once, there was a bee in my face, staring at me eye to eye for a full minute before it flew away. Bees just don't behave that way normally. But what's normal anymore? I think there are special forces at work!

I am a believer. Nothing will change that, and I don't care what people say. Unless this happens to them, they won't understand. Even though Noah is not physically here, I believe my son is with me and I will always have three kids. Sure, this is new to me. But I will always find a way to connect with my son. He will be forever missed, but never forgotten.

21 Kevin's Dad, Tom M.

Our son Kevin was born in 1998. Kevin is (present tense intentional) a fierce force of nature. He is strong, athletic, and very good-looking. He has a mix of Danish (I am three-quarters Danish) and Brazilian blood (from my wife Marlene). So, we liked to say he was a Viking Brazilian.

Personality-wise, Kevin was determined, impatient, and stubborn. But at the same time, he was always the sensitive kid. He sensed how everyone in the group was feeling. If you were too quiet, he would draw you out.

I'll share two anecdotes that give a flavor of Kevin's character: one demonstrating Kevin's force of will before he transitioned; the second from after he transitioned. The first anecdote is called Perseverance. The second is entitled Bat.

Perseverance

Kevin was fifteen days into a 28-day radiation treatment regimen. He left at 6:30 that morning to drive to his treatment in San Francisco. It didn't take long; Kev was back to the reception area in fifteen minutes. He had another appointment across the Bay: a chemotherapy infusion.

During the infusion, my wife Marilene kept buckets ready. The drugs often made Kevin sick. The infusion wrapped up at noon and they walked out to the car. Marilene asked, "You want to go home, Kevin?"

"No," he said. "I'm gonna keep my AP Euro Test."

He meant the Advanced Placement Test for European History. Months before, I had reserved and paid for this AP test for him. The AP tests give you college credits if you pass them. I had reserved the AP test way before we knew that Kevin would need radiation treatments and chemo the same day. I would have told him to forget about it. Marilene pressed, "Are you sure about this, Kevin? Neither Dad nor I would blame you if you just blew this test off. You've had radiation and chemo in one day. It would be totally understandable if you didn't go."

"No," Kevin insisted, "I'm gonna keep it."

"Can I at least get you something to eat before you go?" Marilene pleaded.

"Thanks, Mom. But I just can't." Kevin couldn't eat for hours after chemo. Marilene knew this but had to try.

And so, after waking at the crack of dawn, after a searing radiation treatment, after a ravaging chemo infusion, with the retching that went with it, having not eaten that day, Kevin was dropped off at the school for the AP Euro test that afternoon. It would last three hours.

And he passed that test, too.

Bat

Kevin has a cocky, playful side. And I say "has"–in the present tense,

21 Kevin's Dad, Tom M.

again–because it continues to show up.

One September evening 15 months after Kevin passed over, something outside the window overlooking our deck caught my eye. I looked over. It was dusk.

A bat wheeled and circled around the oak tree which grew through our deck. We had lived in this house for 18 months without seeing one. I watched it for three or four minutes. It dipped and whipped this way and that, lapping that oak dozens of times. I have seen bats flying before. I get a kick out of their sharp turns. But that bat flew with abandon, with joy. Joy was the word that kept popping into mind. "Look at meeeeeee! Look what I can dooooooo!"

Four days later, Marilene had a phone reading with a medium. No, we do not seek readings with every medium we hear about. But a friend we trust had referred us, so we booked her.

Kevin came through repeatedly. At one point, the medium said, "I'm getting a bat or bats. Have you seen any bats lately?" Marilene said yes, we had seen one four nights before. "That's him, Kevin says," shared the medium. "He says he sent the bat as a message."

Kevin passed away in 2018 after a three-year battle with sarcoma. He was twice in remission. But it came back. He suffered the ravages of toxic chemotherapy–three times. He lost his hair–three times. He had to take make-up classes. He lost a season of football. He passed just before midnight on June 27, one month short of his twentieth birthday.

How did I feel after Kevin transitioned? Incapacitation. I felt this gaping, cold void right through the middle of me, right through my torso. My wife Marilene wept almost daily, and I could do nothing to ease her pain other than to hold her, so that made me feel helpless, on top of suffering my own grief.

We couldn't do anything for months. Around the six-month mark, we joined a grief support group on Wednesday evenings. That was hugely therapeutic. Everyone there had suffered what we had. So, we had a "community." I knew that once a week, I could let it all out. I looked forward to Wednesdays.

However, three things about that group: a) It was 90% women; b) after five months, we got repeats of the same stories from the same people. They were on a looped track, unable to move forward or take an off-ramp. There's nothing wrong with that, but we wanted something else; c) some of us in that group–including me and Marilene–were having experiences. We were receiving signs that our kids were still around. Some in the group weren't getting signs, and the moderators of the group subtly discouraged talk of signs. We wanted to be with others like us. So, we left, and Marilene formed a new chapter of Helping Parents Heal for the San Francisco Bay Area. Helping others in the same situation as us has been amazingly healing.

How has this experience changed me? I no longer give a shit about the material things. I live for experiences and being around people we love. I couldn't stay motivated in my Chief Financial Officer job. So, I retired to pursue writing, a long-held but neglected passion.

There is so much more out there than what we see, touch, smell, and feel. I believe that less than one percent of the universe is "available" to our physical selves. Kevin is clearly in a "layer" of existence close to this one. I'm now interested in ways to broaden my perceptive powers and tune in to a wider universe.

Advice for dads in loss? Get into Helping Fathers Heal. This is the most healing thing I've done. These men are your brothers. We can –and do– talk about whatever is on our minds. We cry. We drop f-bombs...all the time.

Following are some other activities that have helped me heal. All of these have helped me vent grief. And I think that getting the grief out allows other healing to come in:

- Crying. Automatic? Many men bottle it up. That's unhealthy. Let it out! Have private fits of sobbing in a fetal position. Cry every day if you feel it. You'll feel better.
- Doing physical stuff. Punch a heavy bag. Hit golf balls at the driving range. Hit baseballs in the batting cage. Take kung fu lessons.
- Hiking and walking in nature.
- Reading about the spiritual world.

- Writing. It was massively healing for me to write a book about Kevin and our family's experiences. I called it *Relentless–From Both Sides of the Veil*. But I think any writing, such as a journal, is therapeutic.
- Doing any artistic endeavor. It helps get out the grief: painting; sculpting; music.
- Helping others. This has been and continues to be hugely healing.

Let's talk about signs. How much time do we have…? Kidding aside, Kevin has delivered so many signs in so many ways that I can't recount them all. I'll share just two anecdotes about Kevin's most impressive signs. One is called the License Plate Sign. The second is called the Lemon Tree Story.

The License Plate Sign

Months after Kev passed, I had to make a five-hour drive for work. I was debating with myself on whether to hire a candidate. I was on the fence about him.

In the truck, I spoke to Kevin. I asked him if I should hire the guy. And I asked for a specific, unambiguous answer, which would leave no doubt about interpretation. After that, I settled in for the drive. I had scheduled a phone touch-base with the candidate for two o'clock. I began the drive at eleven in the morning. While driving, I was looking for Kevin's answer. I peered at license plates, billboards, truck business names, and even clouds.

I saw nothing. Noon passed. Then 1:00…1:30…1:45. Still nothing.

1:55 p.m. Five minutes until my phone check-in. Looked like I was not going to get an answer from Kev.

At three minutes before 2 p.m., a car passed me. Its license plate read "570 YES." I did a double-take. I read the plate again. Yep, 570 YES. I had read it correctly.

The number 57 was Kevin's varsity football jersey number. So, Kevin said: "57 Oh, yes!" I should hire this guy.

I researched it at home. There are fourteen million registered cars in California (where this story takes place). Only one had that license plate. So that's a one-in-fourteen-million chance that this specific car would pass me. But also, that plate answered a very specific request and gave an unambiguous answer.

I shared this story with other people over the next few days. One of them said, "So, this happened at 1:57 p.m., then, right?"

Well, hell! How did I miss that for four days after it happened? So, a one-in-fourteen million shot, with the precise answer to my request, and it had happened at exactly 1:57 p.m. (the 57 theme being repeated). So, the chances of all those synchronicities happening together goes astronomically higher than one-in-fourteen million. A skeptic could still say "It's all a coincidence." But I know better.

Kevin, puffing out his chest, "How d'ya like me NOW?!"

I did hire that candidate, and it turned out he was a good hire.

The Lemon Tree Story

My wife Marilene put a handful of potted plants and shrubs around our deck. In the winter of 2019/2020–about a year and a half after Kevin's transition–she bought a tiny lemon tree and put it in a blue ceramic planter.

The tree grew to two-and-a-half feet. It bloomed, and the flowers

21 Kevin's Dad, Tom M.

produced six lemons. The lemons start green, like store-bought limes. The green fruit turns yellow as it ripens. In December, when the morning sun lights them, they look like little suns.

We put our house on the market in November. Under coronavirus protocols, there were no open houses; people could only see the house by appointment. Before a scheduled showing, we tidied up the house, and we left for the prospective buyer's visit. When we returned, my ever-vigilant wife surveyed the house to ensure that nothing was missing. She never failed to count the lemons on her tree. Yep, still six.

December 7. Morning. The three of us–me, Marilene, and our 21-year-old son Gustavo–huddled over coffees. Occasionally, a brief chat over a news item or sports event. Marilene sat at a barstool at the granite island, and answered a phone call. Gustavo and I sank into the sofa next to the picture windows.

Marilene, with her back to the window, murmured something about her six lemons. From my spot on the sofa, I glanced out at the tree.

"Seven," I said.

Marilene, still on her phone, retorted "Six."

I verified my count. "Seven."

Marilene grew impatient. "Tom, there's six lemons on that tree." She was so certain of this that she didn't bother to turn around.

"Dear, I'm looking right at it. There are seven lemons."

Marilene's impatience mounted, but she didn't turn around. "Tom, I count those lemons every time we come back to the house. There are six lemons there!" she insisted.

I could have stopped there. But she was going to discover it for herself. So, I sent the ping pong ball back across the net once more, with more zing on it. "Dear, shall we bet $1,000 on it? Seven lemons are out there."

Finally, exasperated with me, and certain of what she knew to be true, Marilene set down her phone and turned around. She scanned the lemon tree outside. She murmured something. Then she hopped down from the stool, stepped outside, and over to the tree. She stood there several seconds, counting, then re-counting. She re-entered the family room.

"There were six lemons on that tree a week ago!" she said, eyes wide. "Tom, you remember six, don't you?"

She was right. I, too, had counted those lemons. And I knew for a fact there were six lemons three weeks before. And she always checked them when we came home.

So, sometime over the prior several days, that lemon tree grew a ripe, yellow lemon. It could have been overnight. It could have been a week. I knew that it had been no more than three weeks. And Marilene hadn't miscounted; I was a witness.

Here, you might ask, "How long does it take for a lemon tree to produce ripe yellow fruit?" I looked it up. Local circumstances—sun, heat, soil, and water—can dramatically affect the duration of the process. But it normally takes four to twelve months!

Kevin has shown up for us in countless ways since he passed: playing with our phone screens; on license plates; with animals; with birds; via a praying mantis once, in a place where they are not common; in visitation dreams; in numbered scraps of paper; coins found in odd places; in songs on the radio; and in strange encounters with people. But this—the production of a ripe lemon almost overnight—was a delightful new sign from him.

But if this anecdote was not convincing enough, I got a piece of validation on December 21. That day, the Helping Parents Heal group was holding a Zoom gallery reading with two well-known mediums. For those unfamiliar, a gallery reading means that there's a crowd, and the medium(s) get messages for selected people in the crowd.

By the time I signed on, there were more than 180 people on the Zoom call. I listened for five minutes. The mediums were sharing messages and images. At each message or image, someone piped into the Chat, "That's me!" or "That's my daughter, Viv!" But with an audience over 180, the odds were slim that I'd get something from Kevin. While still on Mute, I spoke to him.

"Hey, buddy. Looks kinda uphill for me to hope for much from ya today. If it's possible to squeeze in a scrap of a message, how about something about those lemons? Love ya, son."

The readings continued. One of the mediums spoke to another couple about their son. "He's showing me a bush, or a tree. He's shaking this tree. Does that make any sense at all?" the medium asked, her brow furrowed.

The couple laughed. The father said: "Yes! We have a small lemon tree, believe it or not, indoors. And it's been shedding leaves today!"

This happened within twenty seconds of my request to Kevin. I didn't connect it at first. I sat, numbed, at my desk. Wait, what? Did I just hear that? A minute later, it sank in that Kevin had heard and answered my request immediately. What are the chances that I ask Kevin for something about lemons and the very next instant these two parents are talking about a lemon tree in their house?

But I ought not to have been surprised because what happened fits a pattern and a personality. On hundreds of occasions, Kevin has sent us signs. And soon after the first sign he doubles down, as if to reinforce that the first sign was indeed from him. Sometimes he even triples down, sending yet another sign to reinforce the first two. And in those moments, we laugh, we tell him "Okay, okay, we get it! And thanks so much, son. We love you."

The other thing that resonates so deeply about these anecdotes is how strongly his personality comes across. When taking the facts of each anecdote, when considering the manner, the tone, the emotion, and the personality that comes through with each sign, Marilene and I see Kevin's fingerprints clearly.

Keep 'em coming, Kev! We love you, son.

Aside from the signs, Kevin has shown up for us in other ways. Four months after he transitioned, we went to a medium session held in a club in San Francisco. We were still in a grief pit.

We believed that legitimate mediums existed, but we also knew there were quacks and fraudsters. But the tickets were cheap, so we decided to give it a shot.

On the day of the show, the club had a hundred people. There was no way the medium could get to everybody. So, I resigned myself to playing the role of spectator. But just five minutes in, the medium mentioned the number

27, and that was a "hit" for us. Kevin passed on June 27th. The medium spent the next eight minutes with us. He cited 22 items or points of connection we had with Kevin. He ended up 100% correct; all 22 items were spot-on. If I'm playing pure skeptic, maybe five of the 22 could have been scoured off the internet *if* you had hours of time (or staff) to scour. None of the other 17 items could have been researched online. The medium had to know them or be in contact with Kevin.

Near the end of his time with us, the medium said "I'm getting a picture in a frame. Kevin, waving an American flag. Does that click for you?"

Marilene and I gaped at each other. She started to cry. The photo the medium referred to is one of Kevin with his skateboard, triumphantly holding an American flag in his right hand, while his face is turned toward the camera, and he appears to roar like a lion. That photo was nowhere on the internet. The medium had no way of knowing or cheating on that.

The medium said, "That's how he wants to be remembered."

I wrote a book about Kevin the next year. There was only one photo for that cover. It's the one that begins this chapter.

22 Lauren's Dad, Tim H.

Lauren was born on a snowy day, the 12th of December. She was the oldest of three and a busy bee from day one. Her pediatrician described her as being a "Wakeful Baby"–she stayed up late and woke up early with few naps in between.

Lauren was a very sweet, kind, curious, and fun-loving child, with a huge love for animals. She started with an imaginary mouse named Samantha as her first pet. Then she moved on to real ones which included a hamster, a kitten, two Guinea pigs, a rabbit, a dog, and a turtle. But her absolute favorite was Milo Thomas, her first puppy. He was a cute beagle she received as a gift from her cousin's farm in Delaware. She adored Milo, and it was a joy watching them grow up together. Ever the creative party planner, in 4th grade she came up with an idea for a dog party for Milo and the neighborhood dogs. She created cute hand-drawn invitations and left them in neighbors' mailboxes and stapled them to telephone poles. On the day of the party, we headed to the park and much to my surprise, there were a dozen or so dogs accompanied by numerous family members waiting for the event to begin. They were inseparable, until Milo passed away at the age of 15. Fittingly, Lauren and Milo are now reunited on the Other Side.

Learning came naturally for Lauren. She was a good student with a strong interest in both art and science. She was very modest about her achievements and preferred to avoid the spotlight, so we weren't all that surprised she didn't tell us she made National Honor Society. Fortunately, we found out when a neighbor asked if we were going to the induction ceremony. She was also awarded the top graphic arts award at her high school, and again, never said a word. We only learned about it at the graduation ceremony. Another Lauren surprise.

In college, Lauren majored in public health at UMASS Amherst. Under the tutelage of Dr. Lauren Vandenberg, she conducted research on the effects of PBA plastics in laboratory mice. Her thesis focused on the environmental and health effects of chemical solutions used in fracking. She also spent a semester abroad studying literature at Oxford University which was one of her most enjoyable and memorable experiences.

All the while, she continued to pursue her artistic side. Lauren created many beautiful photographs, paintings, and drawings. Nature was a central theme throughout her many creations. Outdoors was always a place where Lauren felt a sense of comfort and calmness, so hiking and running on wooded trails, often with Milo right alongside of her, was a favorite pastime.

She was a thoughtful, empathetic, and introspective young person, what some people might call an old soul. Lauren was always kind and compassionate. She cared about others more than herself. She was loyal and generous and had made many new friends through the different stages of her life. She had a beautiful smile and an infectious laugh - you couldn't help but laugh along with her.

In my admittedly biased opinion, Lauren had talents in a very diverse range of interests. As mentioned earlier, she loved to plan parties and special events. She even kept a stash of party props in her car, just in case! On a visit to her grandmother on Christmas Eve, Lauren brought a wearable inflatable reindeer antler headset and a set of red rings to play ring toss (more on an antler synchronicity later). She loved horror movies, during which Lauren would provide her friends with a hilarious commentary throughout. Lauren was an active and adventurous athlete who loved to play sports; soccer, basketball, field hockey, track, trail running, and skiing.

Lauren and I enjoyed many adventures together and she was always up for a challenge. She even convinced me to go skydiving in San Diego and scuba diving in Cancun. We both shared a love of craft beer, especially Hazy IPAs. Always the thoughtful daughter, she once drove hundreds of miles across Massachusetts to pick up some beer and merchandise from my favorite brewery as a surprise Christmas gift. Unfortunately, she got a flat tire on the way back, and she had to call me for roadside assistance. She didn't tell me where she was or what she was doing until I opened my gifts and heard her story. Lauren always knew how to make me smile.

Lauren had a passion for music, which started with piano and trombone lessons as a child. She had recently purchased a guitar. Her friends told us that Lauren always had the best playlists which were featured in her creative party themes. She had eclectic taste in music and attended many concerts. She especially loved attending the Osheaga Festival in Montreal every year with her friends. They had also purchased tickets to attend a Glass Animals concert at the Red Rocks Amphitheater. More on Glass Animals comes later in the story, and it's pretty special.

Some of my favorite moments with Lauren were the simple, unplanned, spontaneous ones. She had a way of making ordinary moments extraordinary. She would surprise me, amaze me, crack me up, or touch my heart with her words and actions.

Lauren suffered from depression beginning in her early teen years. She was very open about her struggles and the importance of mental health care and sought various approaches to manage her depression. After graduating from UMASS, she worked in marketing at an office furniture and design company that, like many, dramatically slowed during the COVID pandemic. She survived several rounds of layoffs but ultimately her job was eliminated. She had recently completed a User Experience (UX) training program and even created three mobile apps. Lauren then began a search for positions as a UX designer. The COVID pandemic took a toll on her, and the increased isolation compounded her struggle with depression. Tragically, it was a battle she could not overcome. Lauren transitioned from this world by suicide on Thanksgiving Day 2021. The police found her in her car near a favorite hiking trail. Many of Lauren's friends gave beautiful eulogies at her funeral, sharing stories about growing up together. The one word most used to describe Lauren was her "kindness."

The first few months after Lauren passed, I experienced intense feelings of despair, shock, grief, and guilt. I'm sure these emotions are common with the passing of a child, but for me they seemed to be amplified by her decision to take her own life, which added yet another layer of pain, confusion, and questions. I cried every day for the first six months. Harder still are all the would've, could've, should've thoughts and ruminations of the missed signs and red flags; these thoughts still consume me to this day.

My wife, Teresa, discovered the Helping Parents Heal group on Facebook, and it has been a tremendous source of support for us. We attended the HPH conference in Phoenix in 2022 and were introduced to the concept of becoming "Shining Light Parents." The idea is to celebrate the life and the eternal spirit that was–and is–your child. HPH embraces the idea that our children are still right here, and we can find ways to connect with them. Teresa feels like Lauren was instrumental in making the introduction to this group.

A common refrain I've heard is, "Friends become acquaintances and acquaintances become friends," and it is something I've experienced firsthand.

22 Lauren's Dad, Tim H.

In the beginning, family, friends, and the community were very supportive, but as time goes by, people unsurprisingly go on with their lives. After Lauren passed, I was most surprised at how some of the people I thought would be the most supportive and empathetic were neither. Many people have been uncomfortable talking about Lauren's struggles and her passing. Admittedly, I was probably guilty of the same thing before I experienced it for myself–feeling awkward, not having the right words, and avoiding talking about the passing of a loved one for fear it would only increase their grief. But now, I understand that it's just the opposite. I LOVE to talk about Lauren's life, her kindness, and her talents. It helps to keep her memory and spirit present. Fortunately, I was also surprised by the kindness of strangers and how distant acquaintances can come into your life in a time of need to provide comfort and support.

My advice to a dad who might be new on this journey would be, first, allow yourself to feel whatever you need to feel: cry, scream, be angry, be sad. Don't bottle up your emotions. Second, don't isolate yourself. You are not alone in your pain. There are others who understand what you're going through and can offer you support and comfort. Reach out to family, friends, a support group such as Helping Parents Heal, a therapist, your faith community, or anyone else who can listen and empathize. Ask for help when you need it. You don't have to carry this burden by yourself. Third, there's no right or wrong way to grieve. Your journey is your own, with its own pace and unique landscape of emotions. Don't compare your path to anyone else's. There's no timeline, no deadline for healing. Be patient with yourself and with others. Don't let anyone dictate your feelings or tell you how to process your loss. Your grief is unique to you. Your relationship with your child is a thread woven into the very fabric of who you were, who you are, and who you are becoming.

Fortunately, I also found the Helping Parents Heal affiliate group, Helping Fathers Heal, which has been an incredibly supportive community. The shared experience of having faced the same tragic loss creates a strong sense of belonging. Although our circumstances are not identical, we can relate to our respective losses in a deep and intimate way that only those who have traveled the same journey can understand. We talk about our children, our feelings, and our challenges. We listen to each other, we support each other, and we encourage each other. The group helped me see that I was not alone, and that there was hope for some form of healing. There aren't many groups dedicated to dads and I've found the honesty and fellowship immensely helpful and relatable. It's been a consistent source of support and encouragement.

I have also been seeing a therapist and have found it to be immensely helpful. Other self-care activities include taking hikes in nature and practicing mindfulness, which have been beneficial as well.

Since Lauren's passing, my wife and I have witnessed several synchronicities that we take as signs. The first in a series occurred when my wife and I went to pick up Lauren's car from the trailhead parking lot where the police found her. On the way home, as I took the on-ramp to the highway, a large deer was crossing the road right in front of me. He stopped, turned to look at me, and paused a moment to make eye contact before running off into the woods. Several nights later, a family of five or six deer walked through our backyard. A couple weeks after that, we were celebrating Lauren's birthday with her aunt and favorite cousin when, in the middle of the day, two deer–a buck and a doe–walked through our yard. And again, they seemed to stop and look directly at us through the window before sauntering off. We shared this with Lauren's aunt who commented that she hadn't seen any deer in her yard in quite a while. A few days later she was looking out her kitchen window and saw a deer in her front yard; it had just shed both its antlers on the steps at her front door. (Remember the antler ring toss game from earlier in our story?) While deer are not particularly uncommon in our area, we had not seen any in quite a while and haven't since. So many deer sightings in the short time following Lauren's passing were truly amazing. We felt her presence and her love.

Another particularly heartwarming sign occurred the day before Father's Day. I had decided to go through a box full of paperwork that had been sitting

22 Lauren's Dad, Tim H.

in the attic for several years. It was a collection of random bills, credit card statements, product manuals; stuff that should've been tossed years ago. Then, much to my surprise, I discovered something unusual in the middle of the stack. It was a handmade Father's Day card Lauren created back when she was around eight years old. Written on the cover was "Happy (almost) Father's Day" with a picture of her on the inside. The fact I had chosen that particular day and found the card in such an unlikely place, AND on the day before–"almost"–Father's Day blew me away.

I had a very creative sign happen during a trip to Key West when I was invited to my nephew's bachelor party. Key West has become a popular place for bachelor and bachelorette parties. I've also heard people say it's a place with a lot of spiritual energy, where signs and synchronicities are common experiences. Our group ended up crossing paths with a bachelorette party full of girls who were about the same age as Lauren. Seeing young women her age makes me think about what she would be doing were she here physically; I could picture her with such a group. With thoughts of Lauren always in the back of my mind, I noticed one of the girls had a pine tree tattoo just above her ankle. It was the exact same pine tree tattoo, in the exact same place where Lauren had gotten one. When I asked her about it, she told me she got it with a high school friend after turning 18, the same circumstance and age as Lauren. She went on to tell me she was from New Hampshire, not far from Franconia Notch, which was one of Lauren's favorite places in the world.

I'll share one more sign that my wife experienced. Teresa was driving down the road that goes past the cemetery where Lauren is buried. At exactly 12:12 p.m., the radio display started freaking out. Then a song by Glass Animals started playing. December 12 (12/12) is Lauren's birthday, and as mentioned before, she was a big fan of this band. She had second row seats for an upcoming Glass Animals concert at Red Rocks Amphitheater. Unfortunately, she never got to attend as it was postponed twice due to COVID. Lauren transitioned a few months before that concert finally took place. So, the combination of that band's song coming on at exactly 12:12, and on that particular road, along with the crazy radio display getting glitchy…it was all very special. And it's the only time that has ever happened to our car radio. It hasn't happened before or since.

I've only had two dreams where I remember seeing Lauren. They were amazing, but also heartbreaking once I woke up only to realize they were just a dream. We have had a few medium readings where Lauren came through and the messages were on point. We hope future readings will continue to provide even more evidence that Lauren is still with us in Spirit. This is an area we intend to explore further.

In my experience, grief isn't a straight-line process. It's a roller coaster of emotions that can become overwhelming at any moment. A song, a smell, or a picture can bring back a flood of memories and tears. I've come to realize that grief is not something you can control or overcome. It's something you learn to live with and deal with as best you can. I've learned that mental health is vital, and that depression is not a choice or a sign of weakness. It's not something you can "just snap out of," as many people might suggest in their well-intentioned but misplaced comments. During this time, I've discovered the healing value of kindness, both towards myself (self-care) and to others I come in contact with. Finally, I've learned that nothing is guaranteed and that your world can be turned upside down in an instant, changing your life forever. So, I've been trying to enjoy each moment when possible.

I've come to treasure every memory I have with Lauren. I regret the moments I may have missed, but at the time, I thought I was giving her space and respecting her privacy. Maybe I was just avoiding the uncomfortable conversations and not knowing how to help. Maybe I was afraid of upsetting her or making things worse. I feel I also took her presence for granted, thinking she'd always be there. I wish I had done more to help her, to show her how much I loved her and how proud I was of her.

But I'm sure she knows it now.

23 Zach's Dad, Chris D.

One pill and one mistake. That's what took 17-year-old Zach Didier.

My name is Chris Didier. I'm the father of three incredible children, and I'm Zach's dad.

I'm originally from Sacramento and a retired military member with 26 years of service. Although my career has had many challenging moments, my most recent tragedy is my greatest loss. I never imagined I would suffer an unspeakable loss that has brought such torment to me and those I care about.

Zach was a high-caliber kid, successful in academia, athletics, music, and community service. He was a straight-A student, active in scouting, and a recognized multi-sport athlete. Zach participated in every summer camp with his Scout Troop and thoroughly enjoyed mentoring younger scouts. Despite the challenges of COVID restrictions, he was nearing completion of the Eagle Scout rank. Zach's favorite sports were soccer and track and field, as a hurdler. During his sophomore year track season, Zach reminded me of the Louie Zamperini story, immortalized in the film *Unbroken*. At every track meet, Zach set a new personal record, which led him to compete in the Sac-Joaquin California Interscholastic Federation (CIF) sectionals at the end of the season. He was the only student from his high school to compete in his event: the 110-meter high hurdle. His achievements and spirit on the field earned him the coveted "Coaches Award" that year.

During his junior year, Zach auditioned for his school's spring musical production, High School Musical, and landed the lead role of Troy Bolton. Zach was known to be a leader who helped inspire others in the cast to push themselves to successfully perform challenging choreography on stage.

I coached Zach's soccer team for six seasons, and he was one of our star players. It was a thrill to watch his speed and agility on the pitch. Early in high school, he and I earned our scuba qualifications together and traveled to several popular dive spots in wonderful parts of the world. These special times together have created unforgettable magical moments.

Despite all of Zach's achievements, I feel his stand-out quality was to be of help to his friends. Zach always stayed after practice to help teammates with their speed work, tutor classmates who struggled with a topic, or help a new student on campus find their classroom.

Only three months after he passed, Zach's mother and I opened acceptance letters from five campuses of the University of California–including UCLA–on what would have been near his 18th birthday.

In December 2020, Zach was with some friends at our local mall shortly after it had reopened following COVID lockdown restrictions. Zach was thrilled to be out of lockdown and to spend the last months of his high school life with his friends.

None of us knew that drug dealers and traffickers were also at our local mall. They were peddling poison through popular social media apps, namely Snapchat. Zach and his friend met a drug dealer and bought what they were told was a Percocet pill. We learned later that this stranger had been recently placed on probation. Instead of Percocet, they were sold a fake pill made of

23 Zach's Dad, Chris D.

illicit fentanyl.

Zach had no chance. I found him in his bedroom, appearing to be asleep, but not breathing. It was only two days after Christmas. I never imagined I would use my military training to give CPR to a soldier on a battlefield, let alone to my own son in his bedroom.

Police, first responders, and the coroner spent hours examining Zach's body and searched every corner of his room. They found no evidence of drug use (no drug products or paraphernalia), and so it was a mystery. They guessed my precious son had passed from an undetected health complication or from fentanyl. Two months later, a toxicology report confirmed that it was fentanyl. Back then, the term "fake pill" (in this case, sold as Percocet) was not talked about in our community or in daily news articles like it is today.

The weeks and months following Zach's passing were intense, a pain I have never experienced. It was a kind of pain where words simply don't reach. I suffered random episodes of uncontrollable anguish that literally brought me to my knees. I felt completely destroyed and broken. When these waves of grief hit, it seemed like an out-of-body experience. It felt like I was in an emotional rip current, fighting to return to a beach but trapped in the retreating waters. Before I could get out, I sensed another tsunami-like wave approaching, knowing it would be inescapable. It crashed with a savage force like nothing I've experienced before. I felt that I completely lost control, as my life tumbled under the crashing waves. It was a debilitating experience that made it difficult to breathe. I couldn't sense which way was up, and I felt like my life was being dragged further into the deep. It was all I could do to stop coughing and crying, as I tried to clear my mind and body. I could barely stand up and struggled to breathe normally again. The enormity and frequency of these spasms were unpredictable. Escape from this misery seemed impossible in those first months. I felt like I needed to fight to survive and regain some control over my life.

This tragedy impacted our community and, of course, our entire family. My mother–despite having had a clean bill of health from her doctor recently–passed away from a massive heart attack only days before Zach's funeral. She had dinner at my home just the night before and appeared strong and was very supportive in the aftermath of Zach's transition. So, that event was shock on top of shock.

We learned from my mother's autopsy that she passed from arteriosclerotic cardiovascular disease. But I think that it was a broken heart caused by suffering the loss of a beautiful and gifted grandchild and witnessing my suffering, as well as that of her other grandchildren.

I realized I needed to get control of my life. So, I thought of something I had learned during survival and prisoner-of-war training when I was in the military. I decided to start the first minutes and end the last minutes of my day exactly the same. When I woke up, I made it my practice to complete specific actions exactly the same way every morning. And at the end of the day, the last actions were the same every night before my head hit the pillow. I learned that although I could not control the proverbial crashing waves during the middle part of the day (unexpected phone calls, texts, e-mails, and other triggers of our loss), I could control at least part of my day–the time when I woke up and when I went to sleep. And knowing that I had some control gave me hope; hope that the waves would be less intense or further apart; hope that tomorrow could be a little easier to manage, even it if was only slightly easier. And from hope, faith is manifest. I like how Hellen Keller expresses this in her quote, "Faith is the strength by which a shattered world shall emerge into the light."

My faith has helped save me. Faith that there is something greater than us that will sustain us, and honor those we have loved and lost.

My best advice for other parents who have lost a loved one is to be open to the possibility of potential. What I mean by that is that there may be a way we can take our anguish and turn it into action. To help turn heartbreaking pain into heartfelt purpose. I have learned that there is a new calling in my life: to bring awareness and education about the evolving fentanyl crisis. I have learned that no one's life should be characterized by the circumstances of their passing. Everyone's life is worth far more than that.

23 Zach's Dad, Chris D.

No one should assume that this cannot happen to their family. That was my family. My son had no known history of substance use, depression, or anxiety. Zach was simply a high-caliber 17-year-old kid who lived in the "normal range" of doing what high school seniors do but passed away from a drug dealer's deceptive influence. We had every conversation surrounding drugs and alcohol (along with safe driving, safe sex, and the importance of studying hard) and never expected that Zach would have crossed paths with any form of controlled substance. Furthermore, Zach's older siblings were never involved in recreational drugs while growing up, so there were no clear red flags from any of our children that a drug-related fatality could be possible. Our tragedy felt like a Mack truck that came out of nowhere at 120 mph. One that we never saw coming and caused massive destruction. As a family, we felt completely caught off guard.

So how do I help prevent this from happening to other teens?

My advocacy work has helped tremendously with my healing. I have learned a significant amount about illicit synthetics like fentanyl and have brought needed awareness and education to many students throughout the US. There's a significant rise of fentanyl deaths from products disguised as harmless medicine, while drug dealers continue to exploit social media to market the most lethal opioid drug ever created. I've discovered from our tragedy that a new landscape has emerged where experimentation or self-medication is no longer safe. And there's no chance for our youth to learn life's growing boundaries. As a father and former service member, I find this tremendously unfair to our youth. Sharing what I have learned with Zach's soccer team, his scout troop, and his friends brought me to the realization that I needed to do something about this. Zach cared for his peers, and I believe he would want me to share this story so that others may live. I found a way to meet with students at their schools and educate them about this danger. To date, I am nearing 80 student assemblies in the last 15 months, and what I have learned is that I have discovered meaningful connections with Zach's peers. I see in their eyes their authentic gratitude as they tell me that they feel empowered with what I am sharing. And that they want to do something to stop this crisis. I see these assemblies as a way to help "fill my bucket" and validate my purpose. Having a focus that helps guide others through an evolving landscape brings strength to my healing. A strength that can change heartbreaking pain into heartfelt purpose. Mamie Till Mobley said it best in 1955 when addressing the murder of her 14-year-old son, Emmett, "What happens to one of us, should be the business of all of us."

Too many young people are losing their lives, and it doesn't have to be this way. Our children are unrepeatable miracles and truly are our national treasures. Despite the enormity of the sudden and unexpected loss of my son, I have learned that there is a way to survive when we can learn from this experience. We can bring meaning to our loved ones when we seek to convert post-trauma stress into post-trauma growth.

When presenting at assemblies in a gym full of students, I occasionally see signs from my precious Zach. Usually in the form of some of his favorite things. Things such as Snoopy and Woodstock (both from the 'Peanuts' cartoons and TV shows), dogs, and Nike's Air Force One shoes (Zach's favorite pair). I sense his presence and I get the strong feeling that what we are doing is the right thing–that he is pleased our efforts will make an impact, save lives, and secure the Blessings of Liberty for ourselves and our posterity.

24 Jo's Dad, Jerry M.

My name is Jerry McCreight and I live in Phoenix, Arizona. I make a living as a paranormal investigator—a little more on that later. I've been married three times and have five kids, including one in spirit, my son Joseph (whom we call Jo).

Jo was born in March of 1994 and was the youngest of three sons. When we brought Jo home from the hospital, our middle son Jerry, who was just one and a half at that time, cried for us to "take him back."

I have warm memories of Jo as a kid. He loved playing outdoors – riding his bike, playing kickball in the street, and playing hide-and-seek. Jo was outgoing, so it was easy for him to make new friends. At one point he made this a competition with his brother, "Who has more friends?"

Jo was two when his mother and I needed to go in different directions. I asked for sole custody of all three children. It wasn't an easy divorce–I suppose none are–but in the end I was awarded custody.

The divorce affected the boys during their entire childhood. For Jo, it showed up as fighting with his brothers, doing destructive things like knocking holes in the wall, and picking fights with other students at school. When Jo acted out or disrespected us, we did what most parents do in these situations: we grounded him. Thinking back on it now, that feels like it was addressing symptoms versus causes. Jo either didn't know or didn't want to know, how to communicate what was going on inside him.

When Jo was three, I met my second wife, Cheryl. I loved the way Jo pronounced her name. He called her "Cherwol." She was pregnant with her daughter, Ashley, at that time. Three years later, Cheryl and I welcomed Jo's sister, Amber, into the family. Jo adored his new sister and over the years they grew to be quite close.

When Jo was five years old, I bought him a red Jeep Power Wheels toy car. It was impossible to get him out of it. Jo never forgot that red Jeep. As an adult, he owned two Jeeps, both red. Perhaps it was nostalgia for his childhood as if he just wanted a connection to a happier time.

Jo was a big football fan, and he loved his Pittsburgh Steelers. One of my favorite memories was when the Steelers traveled to Phoenix to play my team, the Arizona Cardinals. Jo and I made a sport out of trash-talking about each other's teams. The Cards lost that game, but what I remember warmly was the father-son locker room banter and the laughs that went with it.

Like any parent, some of my proudest and most cherished memories include those moments when my kid shared his accomplishments with me. Although Jo didn't finish high school, years later he came to my house and showed me a GED certificate with his name on it. After the challenges he had endured, I was so proud of him, and he was proud of himself.

The absolute highlight for me as Jo's dad was the day he made me a grandfather. I was at the hospital for the births of his three kids…but I'm

24 Jo's Dad, Jerry M.

getting ahead of myself.

Jo and I were close until his teenage years. When he became a teenager, I thought it was time for Jo to take on some responsibilities. I insisted that he do household chores and observe a strict curfew. Jo rebelled. When I think back on it now, it shows up as one more example of acting out, the way he had years before, after the divorce.

Jo wanted independence prematurely, so at just thirteen he made the decision to live with a sympathetic family friend. After a while, he discovered that some responsibility is a sign of independence, not a burden. Jo eventually asked if he could come home. We agreed on the conditions, and I was thrilled that he had returned. For the next year or so, we mended our relationship and Jo seemed to be on the right track. I would give anything to have this chapter of our journey back.

At the age of sixteen Jo met Katie, a girl who lived in our apartment complex. They hid their relationship from us for almost a year, probably thinking we would judge them as being too young for a serious relationship. They were inseparable. I suppose the thrill of seeing each other right under our noses was just too much to resist. They had to be with each other every day. Jo and Katie had two sons, Kaayden and Isaac, before they got married. Jo was just nineteen years old when they tied the knot. A few years later, they had their third child, a girl named Ariel.

Jo loved his sons, but Ariel was definitely a daddy's girl and was very spoiled. She was a preschooler while the boys were off at school. Consequently, she received a lot of Jo's attention. Ariel relished the time with her daddy.

During this period, Jo worked as a mail carrier and drove a postal truck. While in that job, he suffered a handful of injuries. Some of the worst included a broken hand when the truck door slammed on it, a strained back, and an injured knee. The doctors prescribed pain medications.

Jo began treating his physical pain with medically prescribed opioids. Looking back, I now believe that he was also medicating emotional pain from his childhood. I can clearly see it was at this point that Jo's life started to unravel. He became addicted to the pain medications.

When prescriptions ran out, he started buying pills off the streets. The addiction drove Katie away. She moved out of their apartment and took the kids with her. Soon afterward, they divorced. Jo's addiction also caused the demise of the relationship with his best friend. The two were once thick as thieves, but they became distant and finally stopped talking.

Throughout this time, I talked to Jo and tried to help him recognize that he had a problem. But he insisted that there wasn't a problem, or he lied and said that he was getting help. Eventually, he lost his job. In a short period of time, Jo lost everything he cared about. He hit rock bottom. At that point, even Jo couldn't deny there was a problem. This time, he finally sought out help.

Jo tried to claw back his life. Daily, he'd go to a methadone clinic and receive treatment. After several months, he was feeling better about himself. I noticed an improvement in his parenting, and he cared more about life. He started taking his kids to places like the zoo, the Grand Canyon, and Big Bear Lake.

At this point, I feel the need to provide some context. I want you to know that Jo was no angel. During and after their marriage, Jo and Katie had numerous heated arguments, some of which ended with the police being called. They argued about parenting, work, and, of course, money.

Jo asked Katie if he could borrow her car and drive to Wisconsin to visit a friend. One morning, I received a rather urgent text from Katie asking me to come to her house. I texted back and let her know I would be leaving work soon and would come right over.

Initially, I assumed that Jo was back home from Wisconsin and perhaps they had gotten into another fight. I called Jo's cell phone, but it went straight to voice mail. As I drove to Katie's apartment, I imagined a worst-case scenario that truly scared me. Jo and Katie's history of fighting made me worry that perhaps the police had been called. I feared Jo had done something stupid and had given the police a reason to shoot him.

That day, April 7, 2021, changed my life–and my family's life–forever. One alarming event followed another, each worse than the last.

24 Jo's Dad, Jerry M.

When I drove into the parking lot and didn't see any police cars, I was relieved. Katie was waiting for me outside. When I got out of the car, she broke down crying and told me Jo and a friend had been in a fatal car accident in New Mexico.

In my mind, I felt I had just experienced Jo's transition twice. First, when I envisioned him meeting deadly force after confronting the police, and second, when I found out the real story.

The accident was not drug-related. Jo's toxicology report came back negative. Witnesses said that he had crossed over the center line twice. My best guess was that he fell asleep during the long drive home.

It was agonizing. Just when it looked like Jo was turning his life around (he was shedding his addiction, and he was truly investing in being a good father), it was all snuffed out in a flash. The first months were a total blackout. I remember a lot of crying, being very angry, suffering an extreme loss of faith, and many times asking, "Why Jo?"

I had a heart attack three months before Jo's passing. Later, I came to believe that perhaps God brought on my heart attack to protect me...so that Jo's passing didn't kill me later. You can lose the will to live when a child passes, so having the heart attack shortly before Jo transitioned likely saved my life. If I hadn't had the heart attack three months prior, I most certainly would have had it when Jo passed, and it probably would have killed me.

I quickly realized I needed support to process my grief. I called many counselors, but none would take my insurance. I searched for grief support groups on Facebook and joined a few. Because the groups focused on child loss, I felt like I fit right in.

There will always be the "what if" questions that can't be answered. If you're in this situation, try putting those questions out of your mind. They will never be resolved. We can't change what has happened.

On special holidays such as Christmas, Father's Day, and the 4th of July (which Jo loved), I light a special candle to honor him. I invite family and a few of his close friends over to our house. Each guest makes one of Jo's favorite foods. Everyone writes a message or a favorite memory about Jo on a piece of paper, and I put them all into a jar. There are a lot of laughs and a few tears, but mostly we share the joys of having had Jo in our lives. One day, I intend to read them to Jo, but for now, they sit in that jar, waiting.

I have found a lot of healing by listening to people in the support groups. I know that I am not alone on this journey. Sharing some of my experiences helps. Talking to Jo helps. Having his children – my grandchildren – come over for visits is also very healing for me.

When Jo first transitioned, he often came to me in dreams. A few times, he took me on adventures to unknown, beautiful places: rolling plains with mountains in the background, or an Alaskan landscape with deep blue fjords and pristine snowy peaks.

Jo often sends butterflies and dragonflies. One day, when I was working in the garden, a butterfly landed on my arm. At first, I thought it was a bee and brushed it off. Then, realizing it was a beautiful butterfly I said, "Oops, sorry Jo!" Immediately, that butterfly flew right in front of me for a few seconds and then fluttered off. These butterfly sightings continued. The first Halloween after Jo passed, I was decorating the front of the house when I spied a butterfly on a nearby plant, watching me the whole time. It was there for hours.

I have asked Jo for signs, and he often delivers. Some examples include:
- One day I asked him to show me the number 98. Later that day I was doing something online that required a code to be sent to my phone. It was a six-digit number, and the last two numbers were 98.
- Jo's accident was in New Mexico. He had some guns in his trunk for hunting, which the Highway Patrol stored for me. I asked Jo for a sign related to his guns and within one hour I received a phone call. The New Mexico sheriff's office wanted a time frame for me to retrieve the guns.
- Two mediums told me the exact same details about how Jo transitioned. They also shared that Jo said, "I was the most f---ng awesome dad."

My current wife, Judy, and I are paranormal investigators. We use equipment to measure and detect spirits. Shortly after Jo transitioned, we

24 Jo's Dad, Jerry M.

had our grandchildren (Jo's kids) visiting for the weekend. I brought out some of the equipment, hoping that Jo would show his presence. Without a doubt, he did. We set out a few devices that have small lights and antennas that light up whenever the electromagnetic field is broken by spirit energy. The sensor lights – all three of them – came on within seconds of each other. We also have EMF (electromagnetic field) meters that light up depending on the strength or closeness of a spirit. Jo's children each would ask a question such as, "Dad, if you are here, will you light up the device?" Sure enough, the lights would come on. They asked other questions that pertained to their dad, and it would light up again. They knew their dad was activating the equipment.

After Jo's accident, I had been very angry with God, and I blamed Him for what happened. One night, about four months after Jo passed, something happened that I've never shared with anyone. I believe I had a dream visit from God. In that dream, I remember looking over a fence into an empty pasture as I screamed at God in anger. I then saw and felt a warm, giant hand gently wrap around my body and heard a deep, soft voice say, "I know." Then, He was gone. Since that happened, I have been at peace.

Jo's passing makes me fear losing my other children, or even my grandchildren. I feel useless trying to support my children through their grief when I have such difficulty helping myself.

I have received the greatest support from meeting others who are on the same path. I am grateful to know that I am not alone. There are other parents like me. There is a community of people going through what I am going through.

Helping Fathers Heal

25 Josh's Dad, Andy B.

The final entry for our book comes with a creative twist. This father was given the same assignment and instructions as the other dads, which consisted of a list of ten questions to consider. Andy decided to begin the assignment by writing the following love letter to his son in Spirit.

My Sweet Man,

You and I met for the first time at 8:00 p.m. on St Patrick's Day, 1999. As a family with Irish ancestry, I felt there was special meaning for my first-born son to arrive on St. Patrick's Day. Little did I know how special.

You scared the hell out of me with the way you came into this world–an emergency C-Section because your heart had stopped beating after two days of induced labor. As my first child, I had no idea what to expect. Seeing you arrive surgically and spending the first few nights in the NICU was certainly NOT what I expected.

Do you remember the first time you and I got to hang out, just you and me? It was in the NICU at two in the morning. You were lying in the incubator with all those wires and tubes attached to you. I was so scared and had no idea what to do. Would you survive? Would you thrive? The NICU doctor told me that you might need "special assistance" when you grew up. I couldn't believe what I was hearing, but I knew there was no better dad for you if this were to be the case. I promised to myself, and to you, that I would never leave your side and we would face whatever lay ahead of us.

Do you remember how small you were back then? You were so little! I didn't know they could make humans so small. I remember that morning like it was yesterday. I was standing next to you while you lay in your incubator. They wouldn't let me hold you just yet. You looked like a little jaundiced alien lying there. Your tiny fists balled up tight and a grimace on your face like you were fighting some great battle. I guess you really were! It was during that visit to the NICU that I made a lot of promises to you and to God. I promised that I would love you, watch over you, protect and guide you each day for the rest of your life. Little did I know back then that it was you who would be the guide and be watching over me one day.

Well, you won your battle, and we got to bring you home. You arrived in your new room that your mom and I had prepared. Do you remember the crib I built for you? Fiddle back maple with walnut inlays…it was beautiful if I say so myself. I was so proud I was able to finish it for you in time. I guess that was your first birthday gift. I had never made anything like that before. I loved it because it was made special, just for you. Your mom still has the crib if I am not mistaken. It was supposed to be your children's crib, too, when it came time. I guess some dreams were never meant to come true.

Do you remember your first night in our home? Do you remember how

25 Josh's Dad, Andy B.

terrified I was? I had no idea what to do with such a tiny human. I had no idea how to hold you, how to feed you, how to change you. I had no idea what to do when you cried, no idea what to do when you didn't. I was petrified I would drop you or hurt you or not be able to be the father you needed me to be. I was a complete mess, but I knew I had to hold it together as best I could. You and your mom deserved my best. Your mom was recovering from the C-Section, and it was up to me to care for you that night. After a minor mental breakdown, I did the best I could, and I learned. You were such a good teacher then, as you are now. As difficult as those days were, you taught me how to be a dad, by far the hardest, but most rewarding job I have ever had. I eventually learned how to hold and feed you, how to change you, and how to soothe you. I learned what true love really was by walking the floor with a colicky baby at two in the morning. I was still terrified–that never really went away. But I was learning.

Do you remember your first plane ride? When we took you to your Grammy Anne and Papa Joe's house in Idaho? You did so well! No colic on that flight, thank God! You seemed to really enjoy the trip. On the flight, you met a complete stranger who took one look at you and announced to us that you were an "Indigo Child", and that we are very blessed to have such a child. Do you remember that? What was her name? I wish now that I had talked to her more. I wish I knew what an Indigo Child was and what she meant by her comment. I forgot about what she said almost immediately. I actually thought she was a bit crazy at the time. What the hell is an Indigo Child? I wouldn't know until after you transitioned 20 years later.

An Indigo Child is said to have a rich, royal blue-purple aura. It's unlike the aura of "normal" people, which is typically the other colors of the rainbow. An Indigo Child is said to be an old or ancient soul that is highly intelligent, powerfully physic, creative, driven, non-conforming, highly sensitive, passionate, and easily frustrated with the status quo. The mission of Indigo Children, as I understand it now, is to guide us into a more spiritually aware state. Indigo Children are the harbingers of humanity's next level of evolution, a spiritual evolution. I am not so sure about the spiritual evolution of humanity, but you certainly guided me in my own spiritual evolution. So, as far as I am concerned, you succeeded in your mission to drive me to a new understanding and new knowing of this side of the veil, and an awareness of what "home" truly is.

But I am getting ahead of myself. I didn't learn any of those things until after you went back home, as you know. Do you remember the butterfly garden we visited on our trip to Seattle? I have pictures of that trip that I look at almost every day. The picture of you on the train with that huge smile and those bright eyes. That is how I picture you now. In a constant state of joy, connection, and wonder. I imagine you surrounded by all those butterflies, with hummingbirds everywhere. Is that how it is in heaven? I would love to see what you see. Just like on that trip. So many firsts on that trip. Your first train ride. Your first trip just you and me. Your first time in Seattle and your first cotton candy. Your first time seeing Star Wars props in real life. Remember the hotel where you could see the Space Needle from our room? It was like we were sleeping right underneath it! So much fun.

Remember when I took you to the place where I'd grown up? The apartment right next to Puget Sound? Wasn't that beach amazing! All those huge driftwood logs we played on and all the smelly seaweed. I was seven years old when my mom and I moved to that apartment, the same age you were when I took you there. I loved that you and I played on the same beach that I had played on all those years ago.

Remember the "Big Brick Wall?" I loved that you got to see my favorite place in the world. That place holds so many beautiful memories for me, even now. I think it's amazing that during my first guided meditation with Kat Baillie, you took me back there. I loved how we sat together again on those big logs, and you just sat with me while I cried. You brought back those pictures of us playing and laughing together to my mind, and you just sat with me with that big, beautiful smile of yours, reassuring me that everything was going to be okay. I love that even today when I meditate and try to connect with you, you always meet me on that beach. I am sure you do that for me because you know how special that place is to me. It was the first and last

25 Josh's Dad, Andy B.

place I would know peace when I was a child. Even now, as I am writing this to you, we are together again on that beach, and we are running and giggling and playing together in my mind. It's like we're both there and together again. Maybe we are. That would not be too much for an Indigo Kid like yourself, as I understand it.

Speaking of Indigo Kid, are you an indigo kid, indigo man, indigo soul, or just an ancient soul...what do I call you now? I now know what that stranger meant when she saw who you really were all those years ago. It all makes perfect sense to me now. Of course, you were an Indigo Child. I knew then, and I certainly know now that you are an old soul–just in the way you approached this world and those around you. The way you would befriend the new kid in school that no one would talk to. The way you would eat lunch with the lonely kids. The way that you loved your cats–really, any animal. The fact that you loved anything "retro" makes perfect sense to me now. You were comfortable with old technology, as well as the cutting edge.

It doesn't surprise me anymore what a powerful communicator you have been since you passed. I think your old indigo soul just knows how to do what you do because this wasn't your first time around the block. I realize now that your highly driven and creative mind was just part of who you are at a soul level. I wish I had understood that while you were here physically. Maybe I could have understood your idiosyncrasies better. Maybe been a better father for you in some deeper way.

Now, I better understand your mission in this life as my Indigo Child. Your life and your transition, among lots of other things, were to teach and guide me to the next step of my spiritual evolution. You taught me the greatest lessons that I needed to learn. You taught me how to love unconditionally. You taught me what true pain feels like, and what true strength really looks like. You woke me from my slumber and showed me what really matters in life. You taught me about true perseverance. You taught me who I really am inside, the "me" that only you and I can truly see. You taught me how to be a dad and how to be a good man. You taught me what love really means. Thank you, my sweet man. Thank you for all you are and all you have taught me. I am humbled and honored to be your father in this life, and I look forward to when we can play together again on our beach on the shores of Puget Sound.

I love you, my sweet Man.

There were three main things that have made a huge difference to me in my journey to become a Shining Light Dad. The first and most significant was learning that death is not the end. Love never dies and just because my son's mission on this side was over, doesn't mean that my relationship with him had to be over. I learned with the help of psychic mediums, such as Kat Baillie, Isabella Johnson, Gordon Smith, and Susan Giesemann, that Josh is always with me and really only a thought away. The fact that all these teachers were able to provide me with undeniable proof that Josh is active and aware of my everyday life really changed my worldview and my understanding of what we call death. I was as skeptical as the next person prior to my first meeting with an evidential medium. The proof that Josh provided was unassailable. Over the course of 15 readings from scientifically vetted mediums, Josh has supplied evidence that has done nothing more than assure me that he is right here. All our children are. There is no doubt in my mind. I understand more about life with the passing of my son than I ever did before.

Another resource to me on my grief journey has been the non-profit organization; Helping Parents Heal, and more specifically, the Helping Fathers Heal affiliate group. I joined six months after Josh's passing when the group was still very small. But what I noticed immediately was what a warm and welcoming environment Mike Edwards (author of Chapter 14) had created in this group. I was able to stop acting strong and I was able to cry, really cry, in front of other people. It was through Helping Fathers Heal that I learned so much about what I was experiencing but had no words for. I was surrounded by men further down the road than myself, and they came alongside me and held me in all my brokenness and pain. The group is still like that, maybe even more so now. If it weren't for this group of men, I don't really know how I would have survived. I will always be eternally grateful to

25 Josh's Dad, Andy B.

all the dads I have met in Helping Fathers Heal.

Sharing my story has also been important. To share what I am feeling and what I've learned with other hurting people helps me and heals me. When the timing was right, I created an account on TikTok under the handle, *Dadsgrieve2*. As an introvert, I was uncomfortable sharing my pain, observations, and thoughts on such a large stage. The page was initially started as a way to talk to other men about child loss and grief. It turned out to be for anyone dealing with grief. That experience of telling my story was hugely liberating. I was able to really share whatever was on my mind at the moment. I wasn't doing it to build a following or sell anything. I did it for myself and for other hurting people. Sharing those posts had an amazing healing effect on me, and I am so glad I did it. I don't post much anymore because currently I am in the process of dealing with a cancer diagnosis—and all that entails. Who knows, maybe after I have kicked cancer's butt, I will share that journey, as well.

Like I say on my TikTok posts; "Be Blessed, Be Well, Take Care."

Afterword
by Chris Ryan

    I know for a fact that I speak for all the various contributors to this book when I tell you this: We hope you found some comfort in these pages. We went into this project with two things in mind. First, we wanted the therapeutic value of telling our story and sharing–even celebrating–our children in Spirit with you. Each child's life deserves to be honored, and each dad's grief needs to be witnessed. This is an important ingredient in the healing process. Secondly, we all sincerely wish to support you, dear reader. You are not alone in your pain, although grief is a very lonely experience. Several dads put it this way: "If sharing my painful journey helps just one person, then it would be worth it." We trust you've found stories here you can relate to. We hope that you learn from our mistakes and find strength and hope in our small victories. It's all part of our healing journey.

    As amateur writers, we authors collectively found this exercise daunting. It took us much longer than expected to pull it together due to the heart having its own timeline for opening up and sharing its secrets. Writing these stories meant that we had to "go back there" and really think about some of those scary raw emotions, things that were very painful to experience at the time. This is a deep pain that lingers. Much like the physical body heals a cut by creating a protective scab, and then a scar, we have tender broken hearts that have been ripped open. Our psyche has experienced a trauma and we've coped with it as best we can. The healing is a gradual, non-linear process. You've read stories herein where fathers have tried to deal with the pain and sorrow in very different ways. We seek tools and resources to help fill the void created when a beloved child has taken leave of this earth unexpectedly. Some throughlines as we go about facing this new reality include a change in beliefs and behaviors. Some of us have chosen unwisely and indulged in less-than-positive ways of coping with inner emotions in futile attempts to escape such as drinking more, working too much, or isolating ourselves from friends and family.

We hope you've learned about some healthy tools and resources that you might want to try in your own life. A few mentioned in this book include:
- Support groups, either in-person or online (such as Helping Parents Heal)
- Grief or marriage counseling
- EMDR therapy (Eye Movement Desensitization and Reprocessing, a proven technique to treat PTSD)
- Mindfulness practices such as meditating
- Medium readings
- Physical exercise, from yoga to triathlons
- Energy work, such as Reiki or other modalities
- Memorializing through community events, service work, or nonprofit foundations to raise awareness for a cause
- Reviving a talent or hobby, such as drawing, music, etc.

Whatever your situation, we encourage you to find people with whom you can be real and honest. Many of us spoke of the value we found in our weekly Helping Fathers Heal Zoom calls. There are probably people in your own tribe (community, friends, family) who are open to the sharing of your heart in supportive, non-judgmental ways.

Experiencing the loss that comes with your child's passing is a wound to the very core of heart and soul. An emptiness sits within us, and it's my belief that the only thing capable of beginning to fill that void is LOVE. Acts of kindness and love can open our hearts to receiving love. This is truly "medicine" in these grieving times. The power of community and sharing compassion is a prescription and blessing. You will never be the same as you were before...but you can become a little stronger and a little wiser with each act of kindness. Be good to yourself, brother.

Acknowledgements

I would be remiss if I didn't include the children, the stars of these stories, at the top of the list for credit and gratitude. In the two years since my son, Sean, passed, I've had three separate medium readings in which this book was mentioned; the first time, in the fall of 2021, I was told that "there is a book inside of me." I had no clue what this referred to. Last year, another medium said, "The fathers are sharing their journeys," and that "the children are excited for their stories to be told." Then, in a very recent reading with a third medium, Sean again brought up the book but also reminded me that it was his idea. He's a funny kid...a tease. But he's right! He introduced this idea a couple of years ago. It's become evident through these and other readings with various fathers that the children mentioned in these chapters knew what was happening...and contributed!

Kudos to the 25 dads who raised their hands and accepted the invitation to write their stories. They showed the courage to be vulnerable and bear their hearts in these pages.

I'd like to thank Tom Madsen, who was my guide, my mentor, my editor, and my cheerleader as we went through this process. He helped immensely, and I am truly honored to have him as my wingman.

The cover photo (featuring our son, Sean) was captured by my wife, Cyn Colip, who also provided a round of proofing. We are partners on this grieving journey, and her detailed proofing was crucial down the stretch.

Additional proofing came from one of our authors, Harry Bruell. His valuable polishing is evident here.

Special thanks to Reese Harris for taking these words and photos and putting them into a beautiful layout, a digital format that could be understood by the publishing software. Reese is Sean's Godfather, so he was blessed with some shining light from the souls described herein.

A final thank you goes out to Elizabeth Boisson and her extremely dedicated team at Helping Parents Heal. She's been a huge advocate for platforms like this where dads can tell their stories in healthy ways, thus shining a light on the unique grief experienced by fathers. All proceeds from the sales of this book go to Helping Parents Heal to support the good work they do every day, all around the world.

For information about Helping Parents Heal and the many resources available to you (regional affiliate groups, vetted mediums, book recommendations, upcoming conferences, and more), go to www.helpingparentsheal.org.

To find our Helping Fathers Heal group, just search Facebook under that same name. There, you'll be asked to answer a couple of qualifying questions prior to being admitted into the private group. We would love to welcome you and hear the story of your child during one of our Wednesday evening calls.

§

Other books by these authors:

The After Journey. A survivor's guide after the death of a loved one by suicide by Jenny and Harry Bruell
TAYA. A case for the diagnosis of Borderline Personality Disorder in Children by Harry Bruell
The Writings of Taya Bruell. Compiled by Harry Bruell
Relentless - From Both Sides of the Veil by Tom Madsen

Foundations:

Scholarships for High School seniors from Zach Didier's high school. Chris Didier has committed to provide four scholarships every year for 10 years. www.gofundme.com/f/Zach-Didier-Memorial-Advocacy-Fund

Advocacy related to the dangers of illicit drugs (especially fentanyl): www.StopTheVoid.org

The Peter S. Salvino Memorial Fellowship Endowed Fund has been created to provide scholarships to graduate students studying neuroscience at Northwestern University. Go to giving.northwestern.edu and select "Give Now." Then enter the name of the Fund in the "other" field.

The Autumn Johnson Memorial Fund at Kansas State University provides scholarships to students seeking a Doctor of Veterinary Medicine (DVM) degree. Visit https://giving.ksufoundation.org/campaigns/15136/donations/new and in the designation field, select "Other" and it will allow you to type in the Memorial Fund number: M47381.

In memory of Ryan Sills, the Fentanyl Awareness Blog. Mike Danks provides resources and has created a unique Facebook page about Flip the Flying Pig. Learn more at: www.drsills12.org

The Nolan Gibbons Memorial Fund where people can learn more about his music as well as NolanFest: www.nolangibbons.org

The Zachary P. Creighton Memorial Impact Foundation, is deeply committed to help fight the urgent fentanyl crisis: www.zacharypcreightonimpactfoundation.org.

More about Helping Parents Heal, Inc.

Our Mission:

Helping Parents Heal is a non-profit organization dedicated to assisting bereaved parents. Through support and resources, we aspire to help individuals become "Shining Light Parents," meaning a shift from a state of emotional heaviness to hopefulness and greater peace of mind. HPH goes a step beyond other groups by allowing the open discussion of spiritual experiences and afterlife evidence in a non-dogmatic way. HPH welcomes everyone regardless of religious or non-religious background and encourages open dialog.

www.helpingparentsheal.org

Made in the USA
Monee, IL
09 August 2024